T0209424

THE ART OF TAPPING INTO YOUR POWER AND MOXIE AND LIVING FEARLESSLY HAPPY

(In the Middle of a Sh*tshow)

LISA BAILEY SULLIVAN

BALBOA.PRESS
A DIVISION OF HAY HOUSE

Balboa Press books may be ordered through booksellers or by contacting:

Balboa Press
A Division of Hay House
1663 Liberty Drive
Bloomington, IN 47403
www.balboapress.com
1 (877) 407-4847

Because of the dynamic nature of the Internet, any web addresses or links contained in this book may have changed since publication and may no longer be valid. The views expressed in this work are solely those of the author and do not necessarily reflect the views of the publisher, and the publisher hereby disclaims any responsibility for them.

The author of this book does not dispense medical advice or prescribe the use of any technique as a form of treatment for physical, emotional, or medical problems without the advice of a physician, either directly or indirectly. The intent of the author is only to offer information of a general nature to help you in your quest for emotional and spiritual well-being. In the event you use any of the information in this book for yourself, which is your constitutional right, the author and the publisher assume no responsibility for your actions.

Any people depicted in stock imagery provided by Getty Images are models, and such images are being used for illustrative purposes only. Certain stock imagery © Getty Images.

Print information available on the last page.

ISBN: 978-1-9822-4321-0 (sc)
ISBN: 978-1-9822-4323-4 (hc)
ISBN: 978-1-9822-4322-7 (e)

Library of Congress Control Number: 2020903100

Balboa Press rev. date: 02/19/2020

To My Kiddos, T&T

Thanks for putting up with my non-ending snippets of mom-wisdom and quotes. Always know how amazing, powerful, wonderful and loved you are. You are light and love and I feel blessed you picked me as your mom. My last snippet: I believe in you and always will.

And Especially to Bart

I find myself at a loss for words. Nothing can adequately convey the gratitude and love I have for you. You've held the companion ticket through every one of my sh*tshows and kept me laughing through them all. So, I'll just say "Love Ya!" for all the love, laughs, and support, and a big "Atta Boy, Barty, atta boy."

PRAISE FOR THE BOOK

"It was a delight, honor, and joy ride to read this remarkable book. Lisa is a force field to be reckoned with. She has woven together research, ideas, sayings to live by, adorable cartoons, and wise instructions, all adding up to a road map for a glorious life. In the world of positive psychology, one of the character strengths is 'Appreciation of Beauty and Excellence.' Without a doubt, beauty and excellence flow through every page of this book. Atta Girl, Lisa!"

—Megha Nancy Buttenheim, Dancer, Author, Inspirational Speaker and Founder/CJO (Chief Joy Officer) of Let Your Yoga Dance®.

"Finding meaning and joy in our life is a practice and a choice but can be really hard. Especially when our world feels like crazytown. Lisa shares evidence-based practices for making life better in an accessible, generous and playful way. Never sugar coating how tough life can be, she shows us how to do the small things that lift us out of fear and sadness and into love and possibility."

—Lois Kelly, co-author, "Rebels at Work: A Handbook for Leading Change from Within"

PRAISE FOR LISA FROM CAMP ATTA GIRL!™ BUNKMATES

"Lisa's authenticity, knowledge of positive psychology and zest – her humor, love, and compassion – is infectious." —Ellen G.

"Thanks to Lisa, I have the tools to help me be a stronger person, learn to love myself first. Thank you, Lisa!" —Peggy W.

"Fantastic mix of science and woo. I have struggled in my own work to find this balance. Seeing you, hearing you in action has opened the door for my own woo to be a little more present." —Sarah M.

"Lisa has a magic way of connecting with people." —Beth S.

"You are brave. You are strong. You are worthy. It's time to embrace your power and your voice. It's time to be magnificently you and rule your own life. It's time to place that crown proudly on your head. Atta girl!"

—Lisa Bailey Sullivan

CONTENTS

THIRD ART: TAPPING INTO YOUR MOXIE

FOURTH ART: HAPPY ~~ENDINGS~~ BEGINNINGS

FINAL ART: WHAT REALLY MATTERS

She put on some cute shoes,
took a big breath, and set out to do
what she was being called to do.

(atta girl!)

PREFACE

CAREFULLY CURATED ENSEMBLE OF THE SCIENCE AND THE WOO-WOO

In the Beginning ...

How does a successful marketing executive, wife, and mother of two, turn into a woman who suddenly finds her days filled with more fear than faith, who walks through her house bored yet panicked, who has *no idea* what the hell she's supposed to do next?

But wait, there's more ...

How does this same (sane?) woman keep smiling when she feels like screaming as she sits front-row to one sh*tshow after another?

I've been that woman. In some ways, I'm still that woman.

This book is about how I've survived so far, including one of the biggest sh*tshows of my life (we're talking Oscar nominee). It's about what gets me past giving up and running away.

I've compiled the survival tools and wisdom that have helped me, which I hope will help you. Survival aside, they've also made the good times even better. Some are based on pure science (Zzzz), some are based on woo-woo (yay!) and some are based on absolutely nothing (yay?).

This survival guide is a carefully curated ensemble of the science and the woo-woo that sees me through.

Let me expand on how I got to this very page you're reading.

In a Corporate Galaxy Far, Far Away ...

I worked for some great companies and some not-so-great companies that paid me a lot of money to do what I loved to do at the time: creatively market their products and try to inspire those around me to do the same. I met and worked with a lot of wonderful people and some not-so-wonderful people. No matter the company or dynamics, I was proud of my work and my ability to financially support my family. Life was good!

Then, the sh*t hit the fan. My last company was purchased by a private equity firm, and I was laid off. I went from a six-figure salary to zero, with a husband who, as a stay-at-home dad, hadn't been part of the mainstream workforce in years, a son in college and a daughter in middle school. All of them were depending on me.

I went from relative ease to sheer panic.

I had no idea what to do next. (I'm still not sure at times.) All I knew is that I did not want to go back to what I was doing. So, I spent the next two years trying to find myself and worried about money all along the way.

Forget eat, pray, love: My life was eat, pray, panic.

Now I was starring in my own personal sh*tshow.

But, like so many other women, I picked myself up. I kept breathing. I kept moving forward. And I pushed myself to do something different.

Instead of jumping back into my corporate comfort zone, I became a certified teacher of Let Your Yoga Dance® — a fun practice that combines yoga and dance moves with different types of music. I'd never taken yoga before, I was extremely out of shape and despite my professional history as an extroverted leader, I was an introvert at heart.

By stepping out of my comfort zone and fully embracing this practice, I gave myself permission to go inside. I learned how to love myself for who I was, not what I *thought* I should be. Through the practice, I realized I had been neglecting my spirit.

So, I started focusing on the things that made me light up with happiness. I started finding that safe place within me and embracing the fear. I found my power. I found my voice. I focused on loving myself a little more. I tapped into my courage and started doing fun things that brought me joy.

For the first time in years, I started truly being me all of the time. And I created a retreat for other women to do the same.

I took my past knowledge of positive psychology and my newfound love of Let Your Yoga Dance and combined them both into a one-day retreat for women called Camp Atta Girl!™

I wanted to help other women who felt lost like I did find their power, self-love, voice and joy. I wanted to give them an "Atta Girl!" for all the sh*tshows they've had to sit through.

So, this book that you're reading draws from what I share with my camp participants (and a little bit more).

Why a Book?

Author confession: I don't get to read very often.

(Okay, I've read a little, but really the only books I've read cover-to-cover over the past few years have been the three books in the 50-Shades trilogy. Don't judge. I only read them because I love to fantasize about not having to worry about money.)

But I do have a *ton* of books. Books that inspire me and that I enjoy reading from when I can.

Despite not being an avid reader, I'm writing this book because I genuinely want to help you and others like you survive past and present sh*tshows. Whatever challenge you're facing, I want to give you a go-to source of tools and wisdom — my own and what I've learned to get to this very point.

How I Got Started — and Finished

Another author confession: Writing this book was challenging.

I discovered that there are different ways to write a book. One way is to have an organized plan and stick to it. Another way is to have an organized plan but to feel free to go where the writing leads you. And yet another way is to write a book in a week thanks to divine inspiration.

My way was the WTF way.

For two years, I would write a few sentences, believed it sucked, would stop, then start again — over and over. It was frustrating. It was hard. It was my own sh*tshow of a method.

And then I remembered a quote I loved: "What anyone thinks of me is none of my business." (We'll get into this in Chapter 10.)

For more than two years, I had been trying to write a book the way I thought I was *supposed* to write it. I'd go to Barnes & Noble to see how others wrote theirs. Instead of being inspired, I'd get discouraged by their eloquence. I'd read wonderful Facebook posts from friends who seemed born to write a book — more discouragement. But I'd also flip through some books and say, "WTF? If this person can write a book, so can I." (FYI, so can you.)

I also read something in a friend's blog about writing that stuck with me. She wrote three powerful words: "Slam it down. Spend just ten minutes and slam it down."[1]

So, I stopped trying to write a book the way I thought I was *supposed* to write a book and just started writing the way I wanted to write it. I started "slamming it down."

Is this a Pulitzer Prize-winning novel? Thankfully, no. You won't be reading some finely crafted, eloquently articulated and fluid prose (although "rat's ass" and "phooey" seem eloquently articulated to me).

What you'll be reading is my "carefully curated ensemble of the science and the woo-woo."

I'm owning it, I'm bringing it, I'm not defending it and not apologizing for it. (atta girl!)

How It's Organized

I also want to tell you about what I'm fondly calling "Turd Alerts!" These are the short notes at the end of each chapter on things I want to "alert" you about or things I want to emphasize. After all, if you're in the middle of a sh*tshow, alerting you to things that you don't want to step in (or things that may be flying in your direction) seems like the right thing to do.

Here are some Turd Alerts! about this book:

 **ALERT!**

- This book may be a little backasswards: I start with happy, push through living fearlessly, tap into power and moxie and circle right back to happy, thankyouverymuch.
- Some chapters will be very short (not much to say – I believe in simplicity in all aspects of life) and some will be longer (I was a corporate exec for 20-plus years and sat in many useless meetings – simplicity is not always a friend to corporate execs).
- Each section starts with a definition. The first few definitions are what you might find in a Merriam-Webster or Urban Dictionary. The last definition is my take, how I interpret the section's word. Choose whatever definition works for you.
- Along with the Turd Alerts!, there is a "Happy Act" in each chapter. These are actions or exercises you can do to create that happier life you deserve. (Every sh*t "show" may have many "acts" and I want to make sure you have at least one happy one.)
- If you're like me and don't have time to read, feel free to just skim this book. If you do nothing else, do the Happy Acts and read the Turd Alerts! at the end of each chapter.
- An important note about "God." In this book, I often reference God, Spirit or the Universe. I use these interchangeably. For me, they all represent a source of unconditional support and love. But it's _very_ personal, I know, and no disrespect is intended. I honor your own way of understanding, experiencing, relating to and defining God — or not. Please feel free to substitute in what you call your personal source of strength, even if that may be Pikachu or Scooby-Doo. Still unsure? Focus on the substance.
- If you're looking for a book that bashes men, this is not it. It's exactly what I tell the women who come to Camp Atta Girl!: this is about building you up, not about tearing anyone down. I have a wonderful husband and son and I know firsthand, there

are a lot of great men out there. Unfortunately, we hear more about the ones who are not so great.

- While this book is primarily intended for women, it contains some quotes by men. If I believe it's perfect for a woman to hear, I'll share it. Same with Camp Atta Girl! and the music I use.

- And while it's written for women, men will get something out of it, too. (Buy it on Kindle and no one will even know you're reading it. Atta boy!)

- Try to get rid of the "all or nothing" thoughts if you have them. Not everything in this book may resonate with you, but I'm thinking at least one thing will. If not now, maybe later when you're in the middle of another "show."

- Here's a word about grammar: who cares? Oops, that's two words. And I'm just kidding, I do care. But I also know no matter how many people proof this book, I'm going to miss something. I'm giving myself permission to be human (Chapter 4). If grammar mistakes stress you out, just relax, breathe and know it will be okay (Chapter 1).

- I've tried my best to reference all of the authors and creators of some of the tools I'm sharing. If I've missed anyone, my sincere apologies. Some things, such as the "Law of Attraction," have become so mainstream, I may not be 100 percent sure of the original author. Bottom line: It's never my intention to not give credit where it's due. I'm grateful for all I've learned from so many wonderful sages.

- I'm a BIG believer that when someone has a choice between being right or being kind, one should choose to be kind. I also believe that in any battle, both sides usually bare responsibility, although usually one side more than the other. So, when I talk about past jobs, past challenges in my family and more, I choose to be kind.

- As I mentioned in the beginning, this book is a little science and a little woo-woo. It's a little bit about what I teach at Camp Atta Girl! and then a little bit more.

A *Final Thought*

Throughout our lives, we're often put in the middle of one sh*tshow or another.

You may be like me and going through a major sh*tshow of transitioning after a job loss.

You may be trying to navigate your new world of not wanting to keep doing you've been doing, yet unsure of what to do next.

You may be trying to get through normal day-to-day sh*tshows, like work challenges, health issues, financial challenges, family dynamics, divorce or relational challenges, emotional hurts or disappointments.

Or, maybe your life is free of sh*tshows and you just want to find a little way to bring more happiness into your life.

Whatever sh*tshow you're in the middle of, know that you *can* make it through and walk out with a smile on your face.

You *can* tap into your power and moxie and start living fearlessly happy.

Atta girl!

THE ARTS OF HAPPINESS

Happy

adjective, happier, happiest

1: DELIGHTED, PLEASED, OR GLAD OVER A PARTICULAR THING — She is happy to see him.

2: FAVORED BY FORTUNE; FORTUNATE OR LUCKY — She lives in a happy, fruitful land.

3: MARKED BY AN ATMOSPHERE OF GOOD FELLOWSHIP, FRIENDLY — She worked in a happy office.

4. FULL, FULFILLED AND REAL — She had a happy life.

5: ENJOYING OR CHARACTERIZED BY WELL-BEING, PLEASURE, CONTENTMENT, OR JOY — She embraced every happy moment of her life.

6. THE ACT OF TRULY BEING YOU — She finally loved herself just they way she is and that made her happier than she'd ever been before.

(atta girl!)

What Is *HAPPY*?

YOUR MIDDLE SPACE

There are three questions that I absolutely hate:

1. Are you happy?
2. How much do you weigh?
3. Do you mind taking notes?*

If you're a woman reading this (and I'm guessing you are because of the title of this book), you'll probably understand why the second one gets to me. I'll explain later why I hate the third one.

Yet, it's the first question that has made me the angriest, which is probably why I've needed so many tools to make me happy.

Whenever someone asks that, I start to question if I am. I also start to question what being happy really means and then I usually get depressed.

"Happy" is subjective. What is happy for one person may be totally different for another.

And no one is happy all the time. If you are, I'm not sure I want to be around you because as my happiness teacher, Tal,[2] taught me, "People who are happy all the time are either psychotic or dead."

If your goal is to be happy all the time, you're going to fail miserably and you'll be happy none of the time. This book won't help you. Life is all about ebbs and flows, ups and downs.

So, before we go any further, I think it's important to understand what I'm talking about when I refer to living fearlessly happy or happiness.

For me, the term happy means being at peace, being authentic, feeling fulfilled and filled with gratitude.

You've heard the expression often or similar expressions: Things don't make you happy. People don't make you happy. Happiness comes from inside.

And that is true for me. When I feel a sense of peace deep inside, when I know I'm being the real me, when helping people makes me feel full and grateful, that's when I can answer that first question with a resounding "yes!"

Of course there are times I feel panicked or angry. And there are times that I feel sad and just don't feel like going on. Remember, no one is happy all the time — and that's okay.

Life is all about ups and downs. Happy lies in the middle.

This book is about tapping into your power and your moxie, so you can start living fearlessly in the middle as much as possible. It's in the middle that there's contentment. That's where you find peace and gratitude.

So, let's go find your middle space.

Atta girl!

Happy Act
What Does the Word "Happy" Mean to You?

Write some words or concepts that bring a smile to your soul:

_____   _____

_____   _____

_____   _____

_____   _____

 ALERT!

- If anyone asks if you're happy, run!
- Realize that no one is happy all the time, and that's more than ok.
- If someone asks you to take notes, feign carpel tunnel syndrome.

*I know that third question is a strange one to hate, but I was often asked to take notes in meetings filled with men. Because it's more apparent now that it's demeaning to ask this of women only, "Will someone take notes?" is now asked of the entire group. Still, nine times out of ten, it's a woman who volunteers. So, always say "no" to the third question or just don't raise your hand to that one. (And always say "none of your business" to the second.)

Atta girl!

FIRST ART

LIVING FEARLESSLY

Fearless

fearless - adjective
fear·less

1: FREE FROM FEAR OR APPREHENSION — She was fearless in her pursuit of a new career.

2: NOT ANTICIPATING DANGER — She fearlessly walked into the lion's den, knowing she had put valium in their dinner bowls.

3: FREE FROM A DISTRESSING EMOTION AROUSED BY IMPENDING DANGER OR PAIN, WHETHER THREAT IS REAL OR IMAGINED — She walked fearlessly into the unknown, knowing that any challenges were mostly ones she created on her own.

4: FREE FROM BEING AFRAID, EXPECTING THE WORST — She knew that everything was going to be OK and faced the future fearlessly.

(atta girl!)

Living

living - adjective or noun

1: HAVING LIFE, ACTIVE, FUNCTIONING — She was living in Texas.

2: EXHIBITING THE LIFE OR MOTION OF NATURE, NATURAL — She loved trees, they gave her a sense of living in safety, power and grounding.

3: VIVID, TRUE TO LIFE — She is living her life in full color.

4: MEANS OF SUBSISTENCE, LIVELIHOOD — She earned a living doing what she loved.

5: FULL OF LIFE, VIGOR, FAITH — She was living proof that you can become happier when you have faith.

6: FAITH — She was living in the knowing that grace was with her at all times.

(atta girl!)

Living
Fearlessly

You being you and loving every minute of it.

**1: HAVING TOTAL FAITH THAT ALL IS OK SO YOU
CAN FINALLY BE WHO YOU WERE BORN TO BE —
She faced every challenge with a smile on her face,
fire in her soul and grace in her heart.**

(atta girl!)

Living Fearlessly

Are You Really Living?

When you're going through change, when you're sitting through a sh*tshow, fear can take control of you.

When anything changes, there's always a time when it feels raw and scary. It feels like you're never going to get out of the deep hole you feel like you're in. Day after day, all you want is a sense of peace, a sense of safety. You just want to breathe that huge sigh of relief.

Feeling safe and secure is a big need for women. If you don't feel safe, it's hard to live the life you were meant to live.

>Living fearlessly starts with feeling safe.
>Feeling safe starts with having faith.
>And having faith starts with feeling grounded.
>And feeling grounded is the foundation for everything.

In this first section, I'm going to give you ways to deal with fear. I'm also going to share how I *try* to keep faith during those times when it feels like fear is going to suffocate me.

I want to show you how to start living fearlessly despite feeling unsafe and whatever sh*tshow you're going through.

Happy Act
Defining Your Fears

Often the things we're the most frightened about aren't even true or may not even happen.

In this exercise, let's see what you're fearful of and if it really rings true.

As you start to figure out what is holding you back from living, ask this question: Is this really something I need to be afraid of?

Write down what you're afraid of. Next to it, write down if it's true.

My Fears   What Is the Worst That Could Happen?

_____   _____

_____   _____

_____   _____

_____   _____

As you look at your fears, consider if you've had any of the same fears before. What was the worst thing that actually happened?

No matter what happened before, you're still here. You're still alive. You've found that foundation of safety somewhere.

You're on your way to living fearlessly.

Atta girl!

 **ALERT!**

- If you really want to start living, tap into your faith — that knowing that all will work out just as it should.
- Faith is an individual concept. Faith is like "happy" in that it's subjective and different for many. Having faith can mean whatever you want it to mean. Do I have faith all the time? Heck no. Like happiness, it ebbs and flows. I'm envious of those who are walking in faith all the time. I'm not one of them.
- If you're struggling with faith, or if you have "lost all faith" as the saying goes, you will still find many nuggets in this book helpful. If you have faith in nothing, this book may at least help you find a little faith in yourself.
- It will be okay. Really.

JUST
breathe

She realized every breath
was a chance for a new beginning.

(atta girl!)

CHAPTER 1

EVERYTHING STARTS WITH A FOUNDATION: JUST BREATHE

"Fear and breath cannot live in the same place."
—Megha Nancy Buttenheim

Losing a job sucks.
Going through a divorce sucks.
Dealing with a dysfunctional family sucks.
Grieving the loss of a loved one sucks.

Feeling scared sucks.

In my experience, one of *the* most important things for a woman to feel is a sense of safety, that there is something solid to stand on and everything is going to be okay. Feeling safe is also the foundation of being happy.

But when you're in the middle of a sh*tshow, the fear and panic can overwhelm you. It can feel like there's nowhere safe to stand.

The key word is "foundation."

You've probably heard over and over that we must connect with God or Spirit to be truly happy. While I agree with that, I also believe that before you can start looking upward, outward or within, you must have a solid foundation beneath you.

Think about it: A tall building starts with a foundation. A successful business starts with the foundation of a business plan. A strong family starts with a foundation of beliefs and practices.

In my experience, this is the same for women.

So, when you feel unsafe, in the middle of a sh*tshow, and not knowing what to do, find your foundation.

Feel the foundation of the earth beneath your feet. Know that you have something solid to stand on.

And just breathe.

Everything starts with the breath. Your life in this world begins with your first breath. That moment you discover you're in love begins with a breath. A whisper begins with a breath.

Feeling safe begins with a breath, too.

Breathing connects you to your core. It gives you something solid to stand on. It's the beginning of everything you want to do in life. It's the foundation.

One of my favorite quotes is a quote on faith. It's a Patrick Overton quote that I first heard on *"The Oprah Winfrey Show"*:

> "When you walk to the edge of all the light you have and take that first step into the darkness of the unknown, you must believe that one of two things will happen. There will be something solid for you to stand upon or you will be taught to fly."

Before a bird starts to fly, she's sitting on something solid like a branch. It's that branch that helps propel her into flight. Before you can step off and fly and become who you are truly meant to become, you need to first feel that ground or "branch" under your own feet.

When I was working as an exec and my employees were facing a stressful situation with our company or a client, I would get them all together and tell them to just breathe. When they did, I could feel the shift in the energy in the room.

When my kids are having a rough time or are starting to worry, I tell them to just breathe. When they do, I can feel the shift in their energy.

And when I went through the sh*tshow of being laid off, remembering to just breathe helped me shift my energy, too.

Being laid off is like a friend dying. I went through all the stages: shock, sadness, anger, denial, and acceptance (and I still have moments of anger and shock). I spent those first few mornings after in utter panic. I'd go to bed in a panic and wake up every day in a panic.

It was putting my feet firmly on the ground and just breathing that began to help me feel safe, secure, and trusting that everything was going to be okay. When I sat quietly and breathed for just ten minutes, I could feel my energy shift.

When you feel the earth beneath your feet, when you breathe into the safety of being okay, you start the process of coming home to who you really are.

That's why at Camp Atta Girl!, sitting quietly and breathing is the very first and last thing we do. It's also why it's the first chapter in this book.

While just being and breathing can be the hardest thing for you to do, it's also the most important thing for you to do.

Just breathe.

Atta girl!

Happy Act
How to Breathe

You may be thinking this is nuts. You're already breathing, right?

But this is breathing on and with purpose.

Some call it mindfulness or meditating. I call it breathing.

If you get frustrated or confused, here's a simple, ten-minute practice:

- Sit on a straight-backed chair. If you wish, get one or two cushions and sit closer to the floor. Do whatever makes you feel the most comfortable, even laying down on your bed.
- Plant your feet firmly on the ground. If you're not able to do that, connect some part of your body with a chair or the ground. Something solid.

- Close your eyes and focus on your breath. Focus on the sensations of air flowing into your nose and out of your mouth or focus on your belly rising and falling as you inhale and exhale.
- If you're able to, breathe deeply. Count to four as you inhale through your nose. Count to eight as you exhale through your mouth, making the exhale longer than the inhale. When you're exhaling, empty your "home" of all the air, so that fresh air can enter on the inhale.
- If your mind starts to think of something else or race, embrace the thought without judging. Don't beat yourself up because you can't stay focused on "nothing." Just gently bring your mind back to your breathing and return your focus to your breath.

It really is just that simple.

When was the last time you sat quietly, thinking about nothing, for even five minutes?

Make a promise to yourself to just sit and breathe for ten minutes each morning. If you can't do that, try it for a couple of minutes. Throughout the day, if feelings of panic, anger, or sadness come to you, stop what you're doing and just breathe deeply for a few minutes.

Breathing can make you feel balanced when you are being hit from all sides. It can help calm you down when panic sets in.

As my mentor and friend Megha[3] always says about breathing, "Fear and the breath cannot live in the same place." Why? Because taking long, slow and deep breaths oxygenates your entire body and starts the relaxation response in your body.

The best way to relax, clear your mind, and just successfully sit in silence is to focus on your breathing.

Breathing helps you when you're in the middle of a sh*tshow, when you're wading in all the muck.

When you find yourself there … breathe. Then breathe some more. Atta girl!

ALERT!

- If you feel a sh*tshow coming on, walk away and just breathe for eighteen seconds.
- *THE* most important thing for you to do even when all is great in your world is to continue the practice of breathing mindfully each day. Research has proven that mindfulness and breathing reduce stress and anxiety, improve attention and memory, and promote self-regulation and empathy.
- This is a good time to give you an alert on research. That bullet above? I'm not going to delve into all the research in this book (Zzzz). Just know that a lot of people born to do research have done plenty. (Thank you!) Google is our friend.
- I'm not saying that your bad stuff will disappear if you breathe mindfully, but it will help you clear the panic and make room to act.
- Just breathe. *Ahhh.*

Boo!

She gave fear a big hug,
then kicked its a** to the curb.

(atta girl!)

CHAPTER 2

HIT THE ROAD, JACK!
NAMING YOUR FEAR

"Stay afraid, but do it anyway. What's important is the
action. You don't have to wait to be confident. Just do
it and eventually the confidence will follow."
—Carrie Fisher

To say that fear has taken hold of me over the past two years would be
an understatement. It amazes me how one minute I can be paralyzed
with fear, and then two seconds later a sense of peace comes over me.

Everyone has a fear of something at some point. For me, my fear is
running out of money. It's both paralyzing and annoying.

Since being laid off, my fears are totally about running out of money.
I have this annoying fear (annoying because it comes and goes) that my
family is going to be homeless. I'm 100 percent sure this fear stems from
feeling unsafe as a child.

My parents went through times when money was scarce and their
marriage experienced challenges. Unfortunately, that time for me
was during grades five through twelve, between the ages of nine and
eighteen. During those years, I lived in twelve different homes, including
two stints living in a hotel. My mom worked there as a bookkeeper, so I
was always close to her. It was a nice hotel, but it was a hotel. My junior
prom date even picked me up there.

When you live in twelve different homes in nine years, it's difficult to connect with any home for long. Feeling safe at home? Fuggedaboudit! Feeling safe was a hard feeling to find during that time.

One of those homes was right across from a funeral home. My mom affectionately called that home "Coffin Corner." (I loved my mom's sense of humor.) But that's not the reason why I didn't feel safe there. One day while living at Coffin Corner, while I was home from school with the flu, a couple came and took the bed I was sleeping on. My mom had sold it because we needed money. I remember having to move to the couch because my bed was literally sold out from under me.

So, when I was laid off from my six-figure salary job as an adult, it's no wonder that the fear of my family becoming homeless surfaced.

Ugh. F—ing fear. As I wrote in Chapter 1: being scared sucks.

But I'm starting to learn that fear is there for a reason.

It's a fight or flight response. I've heard it comes directly from the unconscious reptilian brain. Our reptilian brain is programmed to help us to survive in a prehistoric world. So, we are programmed to fear anything that might be associated with a threat to our survival.

Being laid off felt like a threat to my survival. It felt like a threat to my family's survival. I had images of having to sell my daughter's bed out from under her. (By the way, that kind of happened, but only because she outgrew it.)

Breathing helped. But one thing that has helped me, even more, is naming my fear.

If you are paralyzed by fear, name it. When you name it, it loses its power.

I don't mean giving it a name like, I have a fear of "public speaking" or "running out of money." (No sh*t, Sherlock!)

I mean giving it a real name.

Give your fear a name like that little boy or girl down the street who used to annoy you.

I call my fear "Jack." Don't ask me why he has that name or why he is male. Stacy Davenport,[4] one of the wonderful people I've been blessed to have in my life, took me through a visualization on fear a month after being laid off. She asked me to give it a name, and "Jack" popped in my head. I think because I was so ticked at being afraid all the time, the song "Hit the road, Jack" kept coming into my mind.

Plus, I feel like Jack is a fun name. I think of fear as being mischievous and annoying, and Jack fits that for me. (My apologies to the Jacks of the world.)

Fear isn't real. He's something we imagine. He's an emotion. And when I named him, he lost some of his power.

I've befriended Jack. When he appears, I have a conversation with him. Not out loud, I don't want to be locked up. (I have talked to him when I was alone but don't tell anyone.) These "conversations" are short: I ask him why he's here and what he's trying to teach me.

After, I give him an imaginary hug and thank him for his thoughts. Then I kick his ass to the curb. Yes, sometimes it takes a lot of kicking. At times, it took me kicking Jack all over the room before he would leave.

But eventually, I sent him on his way.

Of course, Jack always comes back. But when he does, the more I hug and embrace him when he first appears, the less time he spends with me. Fear just wants to be acknowledged so he can move on. Sounds like a lot of people you know, doesn't it?

So, when you're facing fear, name it.

Fear may be a girl or boy for you. (I say "girl" and "boy" because quite often that fear stems from childhood, such as with parents, teachers or other experiences.)

Choose a name you think fits with mischievous, a name that represents someone who gets in your way, someone who is annoying, someone you might want to befriend if he wasn't so damn annoying.

When he comes back, it's okay. Love him and kick his ass to the curb again.

Hit the road, Jack!

Atta girl!

Happy Act
Give YOUR Fear a Name!

Sit quietly for a few minutes. Think of something fearful to you. Then, close your eyes and just imagine a little girl or boy coming towards you.

Describe her/him in your mind. Is she cute? How old is she? Imagine her as that little kid down the street that you found really annoying.

What does she look like? When she walks up to you, you smile. You love her for who she is. She just wants to tell you something. She just wants to be heard.

Listen to her with kindness. Acknowledge her, tell her you understand what she's trying to say. Then hug her and tell her that you have things to do and can't play with her today.

What name popped up in your mind? Write her/his name below. That's your annoying little "fear" friend. She'll be back and that's okay. You now know how to send her on her way.

Atta girl!

My Little Annoying Fear Friend's Name Is _____

 **ALERT!**

- Remember fear and breath cannot live in the same place. Why? Because taking long, slow breaths relaxes the entire body.
- If breathing doesn't work and you feel fear coming through the door, take a deep breath anyway and say hello to her. Ask her what she is trying to tell you or what her advice is. Acknowledge her advice. The more you try to ignore her, the more she's going to fight to stay. Give her a hug and tell her to go outside and play.
- Fear can be a good thing. It can keep you safe if there's potential danger. Where it becomes that annoying little friend is when the perceived danger isn't based on reality. Love acronyms? Here are some good ones for F.E.A.R.: False Evidence Appearing Real; F-ing Emotions Affecting Reality. Feel fear coming on? Embrace your favorite acronym.

She was open to everything
and attached to nothing.

(atta girl!)

CHAPTER 3

BE OPEN TO EVERYTHING AND ATTACHED TO NOTHING

"Be open to everything and attached to nothing."
—Wayne Dyer

When you embrace fear, you become open to new things.

The above quote is one of my favorite quotes. (But you probably already guessed that since it's the chapter graphic, title, and the opening quote.)

I have used this quote with myself, my children and my past work teams.

Whether at work or elsewhere, we have ideas of the way things *should* be. We become so attached to these ideas that when someone or something comes into our world to challenge them, it's scary. We question our worth, feel like we don't matter, our ideas don't matter or that we have failed in some way.

Nothing could be further from the truth.

When you feel like one of your thoughts or ideas is being challenged, try to be open to everything and attached to nothing.

When you do that, you are less emotionally tied to things you are holding onto. You allow messages from Spirit to come to you. Your entire world opens to what is possible. You listen more and hold onto less. You realize there are many different roads to get you to where you want to go.

When I went through training to become a Let Your Yoga Dance teacher, I was facing the biggest change and challenge of my life. I had just been laid off. I felt lost, unwanted and was suffocating from fear. But I decided to do the training because I wanted to do something far outside of my comfort and corporate world zone.

I was expecting to feel uncomfortable and it didn't disappoint. Surrounded by skinny women, I asked myself, "What the hell am I doing here?" I remember sitting in my room the first night and crying for more than an hour. I almost packed my bags and headed to the airport. I have a selfie of me crying so I would remember it. It was an ugly cry. ;-)

But I decided to stay.

That decision was a pivotal one for me.

I talked to myself a lot that night, through all the tears. The one thing that got me to stay was that quote. Over and over through the tears, I told myself, "Lisa, be open to everything and attached to nothing."

That quote gives me peace. It helps me let go of any expectations.

I let go of what I was expecting to come out of the training and became open to wherever it took me.

I met many other women going through challenges. While they weren't the same challenges of being laid off with no money coming in, their challenges also made them feel fearful, lost and not being enough.

I let go of expectations, became open to everything, and I had one of the most amazing times in my life.

Let Your Yoga Dance gave me a sense of self-love and showed me how to love others in unexpected ways. I realized I wasn't alone and that every woman has gone through something in her life that has rocked her to her core. But we remain strong, beautiful and amazing.

Since that training, things have happened in my life that never would have happened if I hadn't been open to the experience:

- I created Camp Atta Girl!, which draws in great part from Let Your Yoga Dance.
- I'm giving marketing and design support to other women who are giving back to the world.
- I'm working with like-minded and like-spirited women to bring happiness to organizations and schools.

- I'm less judgmental of myself and others. I have a newfound love for myself, no matter what my weight.

When you're going through something challenging, like a major sh*tshow, hoping for a particular outcome, then feeling frustrated when it doesn't happen, stop, breathe and say to yourself, "I'm open to everything and attached to nothing."

When you do that, Spirit, the Universe or your higher power takes over, showing you a new direction or entirely new and wonderful destination. You stop waiting for things you want to happen to happen, and you embrace the things that do. You begin to live the life you were meant to live.

Nothing is constant. There are no bad decisions, bad ideas or failures. There are simply new ways to approach something.

And the beauty of it all? If you head in a direction that doesn't feel quite right, you'll know. You. Will. Know.

And no matter what point you are in your journey, if that happens, you can always turn left or turn right.

Always.

Atta girl!

Happy Act
Get Rid of Expectations

Name something you really want to happen in your life:

_____

What's the worst thing that could happen if this thing never happens?

_____

_____

_____

Is that worst thing likely to happen? If yes, then list what actions you could take to prevent it from happening.

_____

_____

_____

How would you feel if you gave up hoping for the "something" to happen and opened up to whatever is going to happen?

_____

_____

Chances are, if you opened up to whatever is going to happen, you will feel trust and peace. Try it, even for five minutes.

Five minutes of peace lead to more minutes of peace.

Atta girl!

 **ALERT!**

- Being open to everything and attached to nothing can be helpful at work, too. How many times have you planned out a project or had a clear idea how something should be completed when your boss or some know-it-all tells you how she or he thinks it should be done? When that happens, repeat to yourself: Be open to everything and attached to nothing. Remember, there's more than one way to arrive at a destination at work, too.
- Save your defense for when it's necessary to go to battle. Ninety percent of the time, battles aren't worth the fight anyway. Ask

yourself, will this matter next week? Will this matter in five years or more? If it won't, let it go. Go ahead, let others feel like they've won. The joke will be on them. You're the winner. You're the one at peace.

She realized it was okay to fall apart.
She'd put herself back together
when the time was right.

(atta girl!)

CHAPTER 4

GIVE YOURSELF PERMISSION TO BE HUMAN

"There is some kind of a sweet innocence in being human —
in not having to be just happy or just sad — in the nature of
being able to be both broken and whole, at the same time."
—C. JoyBell C.

Yes, be open to everything. That includes falling apart.

I can't tell you how many times I've burst into tears over the past two years. (I've aged more in the past two years than I have in my entire life.)

I can't tell you how many times I've wanted to give up. (I daydreamed about running away many times.)

I can't tell you how many times I've whispered under my breath, "I just can't take it anymore." (More than two years of unknowing is enough.)

I can't tell you how many times I've screamed out to God, "Why? What are you trying to teach me? I'm f-ing tired of the lessons." (God didn't seem to be listening.)

What I CAN tell you — what I'm certain of — is that I've fallen apart multiple times over the last two years and that is OK.

Whatever challenge you're going through, whatever sh*tshow you're in the middle of, it's OK to fall apart. Have faith that there will be light soon. In the meantime, it's OK to fall apart.

When all seems lost, just breathe. And fall apart.

Give yourself permission to be human.

Whether it's from cultural "norms" or what we see on social media, a woman often believes that there must be something wrong with her if she's anxious, angry or sad. We tell ourselves we must be strong, so we hide how we feel, or worse, we try to deny those feelings and appear perfect.

How often have you told yourself to just get over it!

Here's the paradox: When you try to suppress "bad" emotions, they only strengthen. (By the way, there are no bad emotions. That's just another myth we tell ourselves.)

Painful emotions intensify when you attempt to suppress them. If you tell yourself not to be nervous, you inevitably make yourself more nervous. Rather than fight painful emotions, allow them to flow through you. Embrace them. (It's like acknowledging Jack in Chapter 2.)

For example, if I told you for the next ten seconds, do not think of a pink flower, I bet you would think of a pink flower. When we try to suppress a thought, it can intensify.

When we try to stop the flow of painful emotions, we can block the flow of happy emotions, too.

As children, we are free to feel every emotion and be human. For some reason, this stops when we're adults.

You don't have to get over it. You just have to give yourself permission to be human.

I first heard the expression "permission to be human" while studying positive psychology with the Wholebeing Institute.[5] I was going through their year-long certification program when I heard this expression in one of the classes. That expression changed my life.

Up until that point, I had to be strong. I couldn't let anyone see the cracks that were forming from the stress of being in a job that didn't make my heart sing, the stress of being the sole supporter of my family, the stress of being a woman in this society. When those feelings of being sad or stressed hit me, I felt guilty for having them and tried to make them stop. It was exhausting.

When I heard "permission to be human," it was as if I'd been holding my breath for fifteen years, and I was finally allowed to exhale.

Peace. Freedom. Permission to be me.

No matter what you may be going through, stop right now. Put down this book, close your eyes and tell yourself, "I'm giving myself permission to be human."

Ahhh.

While You're Giving Yourself Permission …

Do one more thing: Give yourself permission to do something fun, just for you. The key to getting through the tough times is to keep walking, keep showing up and focusing on things that bring you pleasure.

What you think about is often what appears. So it's important to spend time each day focusing a little on what makes you happy, what makes you feel good, what brings you pleasure.

When I talk about this at Camp Atta Girl!, the women usually have a challenge finding what that is. They're busy doing so much for others, they forget what makes *them* happy.

What brings <u>you</u> pleasure? What makes you feel a little lighter? It could be as simple as listening to music or having lunch with a friend. It could be just laughing or reading a book. Whatever it is, as often as you can, take time to do something that makes you smile.

Breathe, focus on what brings you pleasure and makes you happy. If you can't think of anything, don't feel bad. Give yourself permission to be human.

Atta girl!

Happy Act
Make a Statement!

Creating positive statements can help give you permission to be human.

Let's write some statements that you can use when you feel like you need to be perfect. Write some declarations that will help you when the world seems to be crashing down around you, when you're in the middle of a sh*tshow and feel like you must plaster that smile on your face.

Here are some examples:

- I don't care what others think.
- I embrace ALL of my emotions.
- I accept myself right now.
- I make mistakes, and that's OK.
- I get rid of the all-or-nothing approach. Even doing a little makes a difference.

Your turn: What are some statements to counter when you feel the need to be perfect?

_____

_____

_____

_____

_____

_____

Write down a few things that bring you joy, pleasure and make your heart smile:

_____

_____

_____

_____

_____

_____

Incorporate these joyful things into your life more. Start small, like an hour a week. A little joy goes a long way.

Remember, perfection is not only overrated, it's also unhealthy. The more you try to be perfect the more imperfect you will be. Give yourself permission to feel every feeling for as long as you need to feel it.

You're human. Embrace it and love it.

Atta girl!

 ALERT!

- Remember: give yourself permission to be human. Feel whatever you want to feel. It's OK.
- While I totally believe you need to give yourself permission to be human, I also totally believe in seeking professional help if you find yourself drowning in emotions and just can't swim to shore. Sometimes "giving myself permission" isn't enough. I seek help from a professional when that happens. There's no shame. Only relief.

BRAVE

She embraced the void
and discovered her courage to exist.

(atta girl!)

CHAPTER 5

LOVING THAT VOID

"In the quiet, all that seemed impossible
becomes seeds planted, held, waiting."
—Jean Jyotika Skeels

When you're fearful of change, it's often because you're in the middle of not quite being who you *used to be* and not quite knowing who you *want to be*. Giving yourself permission to be human can help.

Also helpful is knowing that this betwixt-and-between place is right where you need to be. It's a place for amazing and profound growth. Unexpected things can come into your life. This is where "being open to everything" comes back into play.

During my big sh*tshow of being laid off, one thing I wasn't expecting was to be mentored by so many amazing women.

Each woman in my Let Your Yoga Dance training was amazing. They made me feel noticed. They made me feel like I belonged. They made me feel like I mattered.

After I completed the training, one of those amazing women, Jyotika (pronounced jo-ti-kah),[6] reached out to me and asked me to help her. She wanted to share her gifts with the world in a bigger way and asked if I could help her create her website.

Amazingly, *I* was the one who was helped. Part of her message and what she wanted to share came to me at the perfect time. (Funny how it always works that way.)

One of Jyotika's gifts is her ability to help people on their journeys with what she calls companioning. She helps people move through the "fertile void."

Fertile void? When I first heard that term, I found it odd, and it went over my head.

But as I listened to her describe her gifts, I had an "Aha!" moment. If you're going through a change or sitting through a sh*tshow, it may become an "Aha!" moment for you.

For women going through transitions or changes, the "fertile void" is that place between what you used to be and where you are going. It's that place where you are preparing for something new and exciting to be birthed while living in what feels like the abyss.

For me, it was that "holy-sh*t-what-am-I-supposed-to-do-now" black hole I was in after being laid off. At the time, I knew I didn't want to go back to doing what I had been doing for so many years (I was the poster child for burned-out marketing execs), but I also knew I had to earn a living.

I believe fear would have overtaken me if I hadn't heard about the fertile void.

When you're in that fertile void. or as I like to call it, my fertile-holy-sh*t-void (FHSV), they say the best thing to do is embrace that time. It's a time of letting go of everything and everyone that no longer serve you. Tap into your spirit and let it light the way. Stand in courage, faith, and trust.

Author Suzanne Braun Levine describes the void this way, "You enter feeling broken, and you emerge feeling broken open. The process is a mission without a goal. We get impatient. We feel frantic and stuck. The unremitting unknowingness is maddening. But desperate as we are, we must give ourselves some slack. We must go with the flow. The solution to being stuck is being still."

You'll remember from the start of this book that it all comes back to breathing. Breathing connects you to your soul. Breathing helps you be still.

When you're in that space between who you were and who you are going to be, it can be confusing, challenging and scary. For me, during my FHSV time, being still was a deep time of guilt. I felt guilty not working. I felt guilty for not being able to bring in money. I felt guilty being still.

But maybe I wasn't quite still enough. It was challenging to be still. It seemed like every crazy idea was popping into my head. (By the way, ideas always hit me in the shower. Why is that?)

If this is you, know that it's okay. That's why they call it "fertile": you're birthing ideas.

Dream. Enjoy. Birth.

During my FHSV, I acted on a couple of fun things: from Camp Atta Girl! to bartandlisa.com, happinesselement.com and more.

I would come up with an idea, research it a little, stomp it out and move on. At times, it was exhausting and fear-full.

But despite all the stomping, some ideas can come to fruition.

As some would say, if you're going through a tough time, just keep going.

Or, for my purposes, if you're stomping through sh*t, keep stomping.

Know that your ideas are coming to you for a reason. One of these things will be a success.

During your own FHSV, let yourself dream. Let your mind go wherever it wants to go. Let go of the things you think you *should* do and be open to things that are "crazy."

Be still. Dream. Stand in courage and trust.

That fertile sh*t will eventually grow something.

Atta girl!

Happy Act
Sticky Note the Hell Out of That Fertile Void

Buy some sticky notes and a white poster board. Hang the poster board on your wall.

When you have an idea of what you'd like to do or create, write it on a sticky note. No idea is too crazy during this time. Each time you write one down, post it on your wall.

When you have four to five ideas, play with them. What new ideas can you think of that tie in with what you've already written?

Have someone you trust look at them and see if she or he can play off them, too.

Have a really big idea? Ask family or friends to help you research the idea. When a crazy idea came to me about buying a franchise, one of my besties connected me with an amazing entrepreneur who had made a fortune opening shopping centers and working with franchises. His advice helped me take that idea off the wall — thank God!

If no ideas are coming to you, give it some time. Go back to the list you made in the last chapter of things that bring you joy or pleasure. Write them down on a sticky note and play off them. The ideas will come.

Go buy those sticky notes.

Atta girl!

Put on a women's retreat

Buy a franchise

Open a combo microbrewery & dog wash

Create a line of greeting cards

Open a Happiness Center. Buy a "Food for the Soul" food truck.

 **ALERT!**

- When you're dreaming up ideas, no one says you must do just one thing. The more, the merrier. The goal right now is to find your way, and do it in a fun way, too.
- No need to play it safe! Let those ideas come to you no matter how crazy they seem. When it comes to ideas, be that Fruit Loop in a bowl filled with Cheerios.

Every morning,  listened
with her heart.

(atta girl!)

CHAPTER 6

EMBRACE THE MORNING
Morning Breeeze, Makes Me Feel Fiiine

"The breezes at dawn have secrets to tell you. Don't go back to sleep!"
—Rumi

It always makes me smile when people comment on the time that I wake up in the morning.

I naturally wake up around 3:30 each morning. I used to go back to sleep. But when I heard this Rumi quote, it changed my life: The breezes at dawn have secrets to tell you.

I started doing this when my kids were really young. As you know, women are pulled in every direction. It's funny, even when no one is asking you for something, there's usually some guilt when you're doing something for yourself if others are awake.

Even though I'm in my office and my husband is a good distance away in the living room, I don't feel completely alone. Odd.

But in the early morning, when he and my children are still asleep, I feel truly by myself. Just Spirit and me.

Have you ever been outside at 4 a.m. and looked to the sky and the stars? I'm blessed to live in an area with very little traffic and almost no light from the city.

That early in the morning, the only sound you hear is the wind rustling the leaves and an occasional deer passing by. (Scaring the crap out of me!)

There is nothing more beautiful and more peaceful.

Finding time to be alone so you can listen to what's whispering to your soul is so important, especially when you're experiencing challenges. You may want to stay in bed, but there's a reason why you're being nudged awake. It may be Spirit awakening you to what's possible.

It's in that stillness that you can communicate with your higher power.

It's in that stillness where Spirit can hear your gratitude.

It's in that stillness where you can go within and find what your purpose is.

Sometimes I go back to sleep if my body is telling me I need it. But most of the time, I get up.

> "The breezes at dawn have secrets to tell you
> Don't go back to sleep!
> You must ask for what you really want.
> Don't go back to sleep!
> People are going back and forth
> across the doorsill where the two worlds touch,
> The door is round and open
> Don't go back to sleep!"

—Rumi

Get up. Listen to the breeze and what it's whispering to you. Atta girl!

Happy Act
Wake Up!

Plan to get up tomorrow when you first wake up. If it's at 4 a.m., don't go back to sleep. Put your feet on the floor, get out of bed, feel the morning breeze and listen to your inner thoughts.

Don't turn on the TV. Don't listen to music. If you can, sit outside or sit in a room with no external noise. Listen to the silence.

As you sit in quiet, embrace whatever thoughts come into your mind. This is a great time for inspiration and creativity.

Journal or write if you feel inspired to. Whatever words come to your mind, put them down on paper.

Atta girl!

 **ALERT!**

- Don't pay attention to anyone who says you're crazy for getting up so early.
- Don't rationalize. Don't allow your brain to talk you out of getting up early. You awoke for a reason. Listen to your inner heart guidance.
- Don't feel bad if you need to go to bed early to get up early. Listen to your body and listen to the morning breeze.
- And for Spirit's sake, don't wake up immediately check emails, texts, and posts. You have the entire day to do that.

She searched joyfully,
knowing the truth was inside her.

(atta girl!)

CHAPTER 7

GOD: IS IT TRUE?

"Faith it 'till you make it."
—Unknown

Writing a book is hard.

While some chapters flow easily, others are difficult to put into words.

This is one of those chapters because the topic is so important and delicate.

I'll start by reiterating that the past few years have been the hardest of my life. My world changed dramatically after being laid off. Jack (fear) has been a frequent visitor.

I searched for faith. I needed confirmation that there is a loving force at work, which can help me feel like things are going to be OK.

Some never question their faith. Others have moments when they don't quite believe. And there are still others who don't believe in a higher power or have faith at all. It's a very personal matter.

I go in cycles. One day I believe. The next, I've lost all faith.

One thing I do know about faith is that you must find it, experience it, know it for yourself. And that's not easy to do, especially in a world now where everything is further from spirit than ever.

I also know that Spirit isn't going to stand in front of you and show him or herself. Not literally, anyway. (But there are signs. Check out Chapter 9.)

And I know on the days when I believe, I'm at peace and feel better.

One of my favorite authors is Byron Katie. She has a simple yet powerful practice she calls "The Work," in which one remains alert to and explores stressful thoughts with four specific questions and a "turnaround":

1. Is it true?
2. Can you absolutely know it's true?
3. How do you react, what happens, when you believe that thought?
4. Who would you be without that thought?

— Then you turn that thought around, find the opposites of that thought and ask, "Are they as true or truer than the original thought?"

I've done "The Work" on my personal view of God and faith. Again, this is my view.

1. Is my thought "There is no God" true? ***I'm not sure.***
2. Can you absolutely know it's true? ***No, I cannot.***
3. How do you react, what happens, when you believe that thought? ***I get scared. I feel alone. I get panicky.***
4. Who would you be without that thought? ***At peace. Safe. Loved. Strong.***

— Turn it around: there is a God.

Each time I question my disbelief in a higher power, I change it around and focus on how I feel when that disbelief is gone. I feel a deep sense of peace that sends Jack on his merry way again. This works for me.

Again, please know I respect your personal beliefs. But I would like to offer that if you're in the middle of a sh*tshow, believing in a higher power or a loving force and having more faith may help bring a greater sense of peace into your life. If you're frequently living in fear, you're not really living. (That's why I entitled this section, "Living.")

This may be one of those "be open to everything and attached to nothing" moments for you.

Here are a few other ways I tap into faith:

- Law of Attraction: Focusing on What I Want Instead of What I Don't Want
- Noticing Signs
- The Power of I AM
- The Power of Words

The next chapters will go into these other ways.

Happy Act
Branch out: Take a Bath in the Forest

Another personal belief of mine: I believe a place to connect with a higher power is in nature.

Since the late 1980s, there has been a practice called forest bathing. It originated in Japan and involves walking in the woods, not as a form of exercise, but at a much slower pace so you can fully experience the nature around you.

Here's how to do it:

- Find a forest or group of trees around you. If you don't live near a forest, see where the closest one is and plan a visit there.
- Leave behind your phone or any other distractions. The only thing you need to do or think about is to wander aimlessly. (Don't get lost!)
- Walk slowly. This is not a race.
- Listen to the sounds. Look at things you might not usually look at. Look more closely at a leaf or notice how the ground feels beneath your feet.
- Find a spot near a tree and take a seat. Close your eyes, lean back and feel its energy going through your body. Trees are so powerful.
- If you can't easily get to a forest, try any outdoor space where you can be fully present in nature.

Taking a bath in the trees will give you a sense of calm and peace. You may become aware of things you never noticed in nature.

Trees represent wisdom and strength. They have an energy that feels safe and grounded.

So, if you're struggling with having a sense of faith, go out in nature and just be. Lean against a tree. You'll realize that a tree will always have your back.

Atta girl!

 **ALERT!**

- Give yourself permission to put up your boundaries if someone tries to sway you to his or her beliefs There are many paths to faith. Each of us has permission to follow the path that speaks to us personally. It's the journey that matters.
- It doesn't matter what you call it: God, Spirit, the Universe, Allah, Buddha, Pikachu. Names are what someone puts on you. Faith is what you feel inside you.
- Being in nature is a wonderful way to connect with a higher power. Experience the calm and peace that comes from the Japanese practice of forest bathing.

She attracted only what she wanted
into her life.

(atta girl!)

CHAPTER 8

FOCUS ON WHAT YOU WANT: THE LAW OF ATTRACTION

"When you appreciate the good, the good appreciates."
—Tal Ben-Shahar

The law of attraction is described in a variety of different ways. Author and speaker Mike Dooley believes "thoughts become things." Author and lecturer Tal Ben-Shahar says, "When you appreciate the good, the good appreciates." And author and speaker Wayne Dyer often said, "Change your thoughts and you change your life."

I eloquently say, "Quit thinking about crap, dammit."

I say this because, during my sh*tshows, I often forget to think positively and quite honestly, want to kill anyone and everyone who tells me to be more positive. Ugh. But I also know that when you're in the middle of fear and unknowing, it's really, really, really, really important to think of positive things.

Really.

Because it's true: You attract what you think about.

Just think of one positive thing when you find yourself in a funk.

Here are some simple steps to help you focus on what you want. Put the law of attraction to work for you.

1) Be Clear About What You Want

You cannot receive what you're not sure of.

In the years since I have been laid off, I have applied for more than 35 positions and probably received around four responses, which resulted in one phone interview and the right position for me. I'm a big believer that the other positions didn't happen because I was unsure when I applied for them. I wasn't ready to go back into the corporate world again. Been there. Done that.

The Universe is not going to give me something I didn't really want.

It wasn't until I got clear about what I wanted that I started seeing the Universe send it my way.

So, if you're going through a change or a sh*tshow, the very first thing you need to do is figure out what it is you DO want. Be very clear.

2) Be Open and Unattached

While the first step is to be clear, it's also important to be open to everything and attached to nothing (remember that?) when manifesting/ attracting. The key is to be playful with it. When you're playful and open to everything, you don't take things so seriously and begin to manifest the things that you want. It may sound odd, but being playful, carefree and open to everything signals the Universe that you trust it to manifest what you need.

When you are playful, open and not attached to the results, the better the law of attraction results become. Go figure.

3) Visualize

Whatever it is that you want, imagine it. Feel it. Take a few moments each morning to visualize it in your mind. See it in your life. Use every sense in your imagining it. How do you feel when you see it in your life? How does this desire help others?

Make it real in your mind. Don't just focus on receiving this new thing, think about your life *after* it, too. Imagine how it will change your world and others' worlds, too. Our brains don't know the difference between what we imagine and reality.

4) Love Yourself

You must believe that you deserve what you're seeking. Simply put, if you don't believe you deserve what you're seeking, you're not going to get it.

Your subconscious listens to your doubts about yourself and sends messages loud and clear to the world. When that happens, you start attracting what you don't want. This is a big step.

The wonderful thing about this is as you start loving yourself, you will send energy out into the world that will help others love themselves, too. You will have a glow when you walk into the room. You will attract people and can begin to share your gifts.

By bringing awareness to your thoughts, feelings, doubts, and fears, you're bringing them out of the darkness and shining a light on them.

As you begin to love yourself, you become that light that everyone turns to in the darkness and you begin to attract good things.

5) Practice Gratitude

"Love" is a challenging concept for some. But love is just gratitude.

Even loving the bad things that happened to you helps increase the law of attraction. No matter what bad has happened in your life, you can <u>always</u> find a benefit. When you find that benefit, your mind starts looking for the good in the bad. You soon realize just how much good you have in your life. It's called being a "benefit finder." You'll learn more about this in Chapter 16.

6) Live as If: The Power of I AM

This is an important one (heck, they're all important) and sometimes a difficult concept to understand or accept.

Because you attract what you think, you must live as if it's already there, otherwise it's always in the future.

This is the power of I AM.

I AM is a powerful expression. Whatever follows it is usually imprinted on your mind. Think about all the times you've whispered negative I AMs to yourself in your life:

- I am fat.
- I am not capable.
- I am scared.
- I am not attractive.
- I am not talented.
- I am not creative.

How have you felt — or still feel — when you express negative I AMs? Let's change them up:

- I am healthy.
- I am capable.
- I am beautiful.
- I am talented.
- I am creative.

Notice the energy change within you. By living as if and using the power of I AM, you teach your outer self to accept the unlimited power of your inner spirit. The things you place in your imagination can become true for you.

While it may feel like you're acting, wouldn't it be more fun to play the role of actualizing your dreams and desires versus playing the part of someone letting the world crush her dreams?

When you act as if, you're aligning with your desires. Like attracts like. You're sending a huge, loud and clear message to the Universe that you're serious. Actions speak louder than words. This helps you feel the gratitude of getting what you truly want. You feel joy and that feeling is what helps you bring more joy into your life.

7) Embrace No Time Limit

It's not easy to train yourself to think only the thoughts that bring you to what you want. You've been conditioned most of your life to focus on what you don't want. So, go at this easy. Give yourself permission to be human.

For some, it will be easy. For others, it will be challenging. The key is to try to focus on the good. You don't have to focus on it 100 percent of the time; just make it most of the time. If you can get yourself thinking and attracting good things just 51 percent of the time, the scale is in your favor.

It will get even easier to attract good things. Soon, the scale is tipped way toward the positive.

Continue to express gratitude and appreciation. You're going to attract whatever you're focusing on. If you keep coming up short on what you want in your life, it's most likely because your doubts and fears are speaking to you much louder than your dreams and desires.

If you want good things to happen, then have good thoughts about what you want. Play!

Atta girl!

Happy Act
Focus on Attracting One Thing

Let's get you started on manifesting and attracting more good into your life, starting with one simple thing.

Get in a quiet room. Sit in a comfy chair and close your eyes. Think of just one thing that you want to happen for you. **Write down that one thing:**

_____

Now, write down what it will look like and feel like when you get that one thing:

It will look like: It will feel like:

_____   _____

_____   _____

_____   _____

_____   _____

Write down some I AM statements that go along with this:

I am _____

I am _____

I am _____

Tomorrow morning spend just a few minutes visualizing the thing you want to attract using all the things you wrote above.

Have fun with this. If it's not fun, you won't attract it.

Atta girl!

 **ALERT!**

- Warning. If you get frustrated and angry at yourself because you can't stop thinking negative thoughts, guess what? You'll attract that! If you find yourself thinking a negative thought, smile and laugh at yourself. This reduces the negative thought's power.
- Don't spend more than three to five minutes visualizing it each day. Your mind will inevitably begin to wander after five minutes. Visualizing will start feeling like a chore rather than a way to bring joy into your life.

She learned to follow the signs.

(atta girl!)

CHAPTER 9

NOTICE THE SIGNS

"When it is all finished, you will discover it was never random."
—Unknown

One way to tap into that faith you thought you might have lost is to be aware of signs.

You may not realize it, but the Universe is speaking to you all the time. You may not hear the voice because rather than a shout, it's more like a tap on your shoulder. A subtle sign that's not so subtle when you start paying attention.

And like the law of attraction, the more you're open to the signs, the more the signs will appear.

Spirit speaks to us all the time. We don't always recognize the messages because they can come in forms we may not have experience with.

People who are good at noticing signs are also great at manifesting through the law of attraction.

I love how Wayne Dyer talked about people who can manifest their dreams and how they feel about signs or coincidences. In his book "The Power of Intention," they're called "connectors."

> "Connectors aren't surprised when synchronicity or coincidence brings them the fruits of their intention. They know in their hearts that those seemingly miraculous happenings were brought into their immediate life

space because they were already connected to them. Ask connectors about it and they will tell you, 'Of course, it's the law of attraction at work.'"

If you're a connector, you don't argue with those who don't believe in the law of attraction, in signs or synchronicities. You won't waste your time caring what anyone thinks ("What anyone thinks of me is none of my business"), as it will take away your connection to God and Spirit. You're not here to convince anyone. You're here to enjoy what's intended for you.

Simply by being you, you raise the energy of the world.

It's kind of the chicken-or-the-egg story. The more you become aware of signs, the more coincidences and signs appear. The more they appear, the more you believe in a higher power and having faith. The more you have faith, the more the signs appear. Think of an infinity symbol: One leads to another and back again.

So how do you notice the signs? The first step is to become aware.

A big sign for me came when I first started Camp Atta Girl! It was truly in my spirit to do so, but I had doubts. Was I trying to do something too big for me to attempt? I did a lot of soul searching on whether to hold it or not.

One Sunday, I drove around looking at event places. I envisioned that the perfect place for Camp Atta Girl! was probably going to be too expensive for me. (I didn't follow the law of attraction on this one!) It was a first-time event, and I didn't have any money to put it on.

I stopped at a place called Camp Lucy. It was a beautiful retreat center with the perfect atmosphere for Camp Atta Girl!

After driving around the center, I stopped at the front office. It was a Sunday, and I assumed no one would be there. So, I planned to pick up a brochure and follow up on Monday. To my surprise, there was a woman at the front desk who asked if she could help me. I told her what I wanted to do, that I was sure this place was too expensive for me, but that I would love to talk to the event manager on Monday.

The woman smiled, said she was there to pick up some files she needed and that she was the event manager. She took me into her office and listened to what I wanted to do. She said they're usually booked solid for weddings, but the weekend I was looking for was open. She offered the location to me for $500.

If you know anything about renting event facilities, you know that this was beyond a good deal. I cried right in front of her.

To me, that was a big sign from Spirit. Any doubts about whether I should create this women's retreat were erased — well, most of the doubts.

Not all signs we receive are as obvious. But when you open your awareness to the signs, the signs seem to grow bigger and more obvious.

Not all signs are the same. There are different kinds of signs to be aware of.

1. **Coincidences**

    Look for things that seem to be a coincidence: receiving a call from someone you were thinking about, someone giving you a book about a topic that specifically addresses what you're struggling with, someone giving you a great deal on an event center on the exact day you want to hold your retreat (wink). When these things happen, you're receiving divine guidance that the direction you're headed is the right direction. It's called synchronicity by some. I call them "holy sh*t" or "wow" moments.

2. **It's Too Hard**

    If something is too hard, that can also be a sign. I'm not saying never attempt something challenging. But if you want to do something, and it seems like things are getting in the way or everything connected to it seems to be a struggle, if it's "too hard," that may be a sign to step back, look at what you want to do, breathe and rest for a while. Problems, delays, and roadblocks may be a sign to do something differently. Research what it is that is making it so hard. Ask for additional signs and see what shows up.

3. **How You're Feeling**

    Depression and lack of passion may be a sign that you're not living the life the Universe meant for you. By contrast, being full of energy can be a sign you are. Notice how you feel with certain people, certain situations and certain activities.

4. **Notice the Energy**

   If you practice, you can feel the energy in a room or building. Have you ever walked into a room of people or a conference room and you could feel the tension? The energy can signal that something isn't right. If you're applying for a new job, notice how walking into the building feels to you. A heaviness indicates the energy of the company isn't right for you. A lightness could indicate a happy company where you could grow and thrive. I've taken jobs and realized after a month that I should have "listened" to the energy during the interviews.

5. **Don't Overcomplicate**

   Signs are all about simplicity. If you receive a sign to do something, don't waste time trying to figure out the "why" of the sign. Trust it, don't overanalyze it.

I'll end this chapter with one of my biggest signs. Around eleven years ago, I was struggling. I don't remember what sh*tshow I was going through at the time, but it was a biggie. (Aren't they all biggies?) I was near Sedona, Arizona, at the time and driving through Oak Creek Canyon — one of the prettiest areas on earth to me. (It's also the perfect place for a forest bath.)

I remember driving through tears, asking for a sign that everything would be alright. I didn't just ask in my mind, I said it out loud and very angrily (sometimes you need to shout to get the Universe's attention). Less than 30 seconds following my plea, right in front of me appeared this tree — a beautiful Ponderosa pine — that seemed to be all "alone" among all the other trees. (Kind of how I feel at times: I'm a lone tree among all the other saplings.)

The sun seemed to be shining down only on this one tree.

I stopped the car and just sat by that tree in awe. It gave me strength. It gave me courage. It made me feel safe. It was a sign to me, sent immediately upon my calling out for help.

Almost every year since, I've traveled back to Sedona for one purpose: to visit my tree. I often write a note and bury it under the leaves in a waterproof bag. Then when I return a year later, I read the note to see how my life has changed.

My tree is such a significant sign for me, that I returned to visit it before sending this book to the publisher. (The picture of me on the book cover is by my tree.)

That tree is my strength, and I carry that "sign" with me everywhere I go.

You have a sign just waiting for you to notice it. When you feel with all your heart that a sign has been given to you, don't take that lightly. Signs are Spirit's way of tapping on your shoulder and telling you to listen or pay attention to something regarding the challenges you face or the dreams you have. If someone taps you on your shoulder, you turn around and acknowledge them. You should also acknowledge Spirit and your signs.

For me, coming across my tree was the Universe tapping me on the shoulder, telling me everything was going to be OK.

Pay attention to Spirit's taps. Maybe, just maybe, they'll cause you to slow down and find *your* tree.

Atta girl!

Happy Act
Create a Sign Journal

The best way to start noticing the signs is to start noticing the signs. It sounds stupid, but it's true.

Grab a small journal or notepad that you can carry around with you at all times. Every time you notice a sign, write it down. At the end of the week, go over all the signs you noticed. The more you notice the signs and connect with them daily, the more the signs and answers to what you need to know will appear.

I hope you realize that you reading this book is also a sign.

Atta girl!

**ALERT!**

- One of the most important signs is your ability to start trusting your own wisdom.
- Some people say your dreams are signs. I'm not 100 percent sure of that. But if you believe they are, then wonderful! Just be careful and don't take "dream" evaluations to heart. Only you know what your dreams can mean. Ditch the dream guides. Trust your thoughts on what your dream is telling you. It may simply be a dream.
- When someone tells you, "It's just a coincidence," smile and say, "Yep!" There's probably no convincing them. But you'll know the truth, and that's enough.

SECOND ART

TAPPING INTO
YOUR POWER

Power

noun, often attributive

1: ABILITY TO ACT OR PRODUCE AN EFFECT — She had the power to change her life.

2: PHYSICAL MIGHT, RELATING TO OR UTILIZING STRENGTH — She harnessed her power to become the woman she was born to be.

3: SELF-POWER, SELF-CONFIDENCE, SELF-ESTEEM, SELF-DISCIPLINE — She tapped her power, and loved herself for who she was, not who she thought others wanted her to be.

4: TRANSFORMING INERTIA INTO ACTION AND MOVEMENT, PERSONAL POWER — She had the power to meet challenges and move forward in her life.

5: POWERS PLURAL, AN ORDER OF ANGELS — She had powers helping her that she didn't even realize.

6. THE CROWN, ROYALTY, QUEENSHIP — She felt her power and true nobility and donned her crown.

(atta girl!)

Second Art: Tapping into Your Power

Dare to Be You

Your power is your truth. It's your core, your center. It's you.

When you are authentically being you, you feel self-confident and self-motivated. You feel a fire deep within.

Yet, so many times, for whatever reason, women lose themselves. We forget who we are because we're so busy being who we think others want us to be.

It's during those times that your powerful internal warrior goes missing. You may begin to suffer from low self-esteem, have difficulty making decisions and may have anger or control issues.

When that happens, you can often find yourself in a vortex of negative emotions toward yourself.

I've been in positions where that has happened to me. I've let people or situations take my power. It can be quite challenging to bring yourself back up.

It's at those times that it's critical to tap back into your power. It's critical to go inside and find that powerful internal warrior.

This next section of the book are tips I use to help me tap back into my power. Often, it just requires me finding a way back to truly being myself, not being who I think others want me to be. Finding my power means coming home to who I really am.

It's time for you to come home. Time to tap into your power. Find that authentic you that's inside. Dare to be you.

Happy Act
Feel That power Inside of You

The energy center in your body that helps with power is called your solar plexus. It resides right above your belly button.

You've heard the expression, "trust your gut." This is your gut. Your gut can tell you if you're losing your power.

Try this:

- Close your eyes, place your hand over the area slightly above your belly button and take a few deep breaths to ground yourself.
- Think about a problem or dilemma.
- Notice how it feels in that area. Chances are, it feels icky.
- Now, take a few moments and think of some solutions to that problem. See how it feels with each choice or solution:

  o If you get a sinking or nauseated feeling, it could be telling you that this solution is not the way to go.
  o If you feel a lightness in that area or like you can breathe easier when you think of that solution, that is your power telling you to go with that solution.

If you find you are stuck with a decision, at a crossroads and not sure which way you should go, tap into that gut feeling. Stop, breathe and tap into your power.
Atta girl!

 ALERT!

- Don't mistake fear for a bad solution. The solution you feel may be a scary one. Your gut will tell you if it's right. Your faith will give you the ability to follow that solution if it's scary.

She cared more about
wowing herself
than wowing others.

(atta girl!)

CHAPTER 10

WHAT ANYONE THINKS OF ME IS NONE OF MY BUSINESS

"What makes you different or weird, that's your strength."
—Meryl Streep

THE most important thing that a woman needs to become happier in life is to finally embrace, once and for all, the practice of not giving a rat's ass what anyone thinks of her.

This is also the critical key to embracing your true power.

When you stop caring what others think, you are on your way to becoming the person YOU love — not the person you think others will love. It is the moment you become the real you.

This is not easy to accomplish, however. If there is anything in this world that I wish I could totally get rid of, it is caring what others think of me. These questions pop up every now and then:

- Is this okay to do?
- What will people think of me?
- Will it make her/him angry?
- What if they don't like me?
- What if I hurt her feelings?

I'm not alone in this.

Whenever I share with groups the importance of not giving a rat's ass what others think, the reactions are striking. For example, when

I introduce this at Camp Atta Girl!, my participants become quite animated. It's as if their entire lives they've been holding this in. They've cared far too much about the feelings and opinions of others for far too long. They've been so ticked off about it, that they explode. It ends up being quite cathartic for them.

I love it.

I don't love that it's happened to them of course. I love that they've had it! Their personal mantras become "ENOUGH!" and "I don't care!" It's wonderful to hear.

The concept of "ENOUGH!" is a big reason why I created Camp Atta Girl! When I was training to become a Let Your Yoga Dance teacher, four components really spoke to me:

- **Safety**: music and dance that connect to the earth. Feeling that grounding and the safety of having a solid foundation for myself was freeing.
- **Power**: music and dance that connect to strength, power, and bravery. When I was in the corporate world, I often walked on eggshells, not wanting to rock the boat too much. I rocked it at times, but not often enough.
- **Love**: music that connects to the heart. Women sometimes have challenges loving themselves. It's important to have compassion and empathy for others, but it's so much more important to have love and compassion for yourself.
- **Voice**: music that connects to sound, truth and being the "real" you. Women are often afraid to express themselves, to use their voice, afraid to show the world their real selves. But being you is the most important aspect of regaining your power.

Of these components, by far, power and voice spoke to me the loudest.

All my life, especially in the corporate world, I felt I had little power and little voice. This isn't surprising. Many corporate cultures tout that they want people to have a voice, but it's often quieted when it doesn't match with what the company has in mind. When your voice is squelched enough, your feeling of having power over any situation gets squelched, too.

It's a vicious cycle: you lose your voice because you feel you have no power; and because you feel you have no power, you're afraid to speak up. When you have to navigate sh*tshows over and over, you soon tire of even trying. You become complacent. You toss in the towel.

Power and voice are big ones! From experience, I knew they were big for other women, too. So, they became the guiding light for the women attending Camp Atta Girl!

So many women are f—ing tired of watching everything they do, caring about what they look like and walking on eggshells for fear of upsetting someone. We're tired of being afraid of not being liked or possibly hurting someone's feelings.

Women are just tired of not being themselves.

Not being yourself is the furthest thing from embracing your power.

It's time to stop the madness! It's time to stop worrying about others' opinions of you. It's time to own your energy, space, and power.

The reality is no matter what you do, someone is not going to like it. You can't control others' thoughts and feelings. You can't make everyone like you. You can only control your own thoughts and feelings. You can only care about what you think about yourself. What anyone else thinks about you is none of your business.

When you live your life based on what others think, you're living their life, not yours.

I'm not saying it's time for you to become a raging bitch — although, that may be incredibly cathartic. I'm a big believer in the power of kindness.

But I'm also a big believer in embracing your true self and loving every bit of it. It's time to be the real you. You know what? If the real you is a raging bitch, that's okay, too.

So, the next time you find yourself wondering, "Is she going to get mad at me?" or "What if I do this and they don't like me?" Stop and repeat this quote from Wayne Dyer a few times:

What anyone thinks of me is none of my business.

Then, think about what it is you want to do and ask yourself these questions:

- Will this make me happy?
- Will I be able to sleep knowing I followed my thoughts, not what I think someone else is thinking?
- Will this harm anyone?
- Is this the real me?

If your answers feel authentic and no harm will come to another, then go for it.

For the past eleven years, I've had the same piece of paper taped to my computer screen. I've carefully peeled it off and taped it back on to each new computer I've gotten. It's a piece of valuable advice once given to me during an executive training session. (Yes, sometimes you need to be trained to be an executive. Sadly, many don't take the training to heart.) When a cohort in the training could see I wasn't owning my power and was worrying too much about what others in the room were thinking, he said:

Own it and bring it, but don't defend it or apologize for it.

That was a powerful Aha! moment for me. It was a gift that I'll forever be grateful for.

Ironically, the end of my year-long positive psychology certification was a stressful time in my life. I was tired of not embracing and loving who I was. I was tired of caring more about what others thought of me than what I thought of myself. I was especially tired of caring what the room of 250 men and women thought about me. So, I embraced my true self, stood up and declared: "I'm F—ING owning it!"

It's time for all of us to embrace our true selves.

It's time for all of us to not care what others think.

It's time for all of us to own it and bring it and not defend it or apologize for it.

Actually, it's time for ALL of us to not just own it, but *F—ING* own it, I mean, *FUCKING* own it, bring it and not defend it or apologize for it.

Atta girl!

Happy Act
Embrace Vulnerability

One way to train yourself to not care what others think is to embrace being vulnerable. It really can be terrifying to go against the grain, speak out, take a risk and face possible disapproval. But decide what matters to you, trust yourself and go for it.

Think of a time you didn't speak up for fear of what others would think:

_____

_____

_____

_____

What happened because you didn't speak up? Write down anything physical that happened and how you felt mentally:

_____

_____

_____

_____

_____

What's the <u>worst</u> thing that could have happened if you had spoken up?

_____

_____

_____

_____

_____

Chances are, "the worst thing" is not that bad after all. We often care so much about imaginary outcomes that we don't show our true selves.

Let's say the worst-case scenario *did* happen. You're still here. You're still reading this book. You're still living.

Taking chances at being yourself and being vulnerable enough to be the real you help you grow and take more chances. We learn to be ourselves by being our real selves.

Start being your real self. Start wowing yourself more than wowing others.

Atta girl!

 **ALERT!**

- When you decide to do something that embraces your true self and not to care what anyone thinks, make sure that what you plan to do doesn't harm another person. That's the one caveat. Yes, they may not like it. Yes, you may hurt their feelings. That's okay. What isn't OK is actual harm. You always want to be kind, especially to yourself.

- What anyone thinks of you is none of your business. What's also none of your business is what you think of others. Be careful! Often the reason why we care so much about what others think is that we have our own judgmental side. Try your best to stop judging and caring what others do. Fill your heart with compassion instead of judgment.

- You would probably care a lot less about what others think about you if you really knew how little others *actually* think about you. Everyone has enough to occupy their mind. They also have their own insecurities. If you're worried about how you come across, they're probably worrying the same about themselves.

She stopped comparing
and realized her true nobility.

(atta girl!)

CHAPTER 11

STOP COMPARING!

> "A flower does not think of competing to the
> flower next to it. It just blooms."
> —Zen Shin

The sister to "what anyone thinks of me is none of my business" is "who others are is none of my business."

Stop comparing!

Until you can stop comparing yourself to others and caring what others think about you, you're never going to be who YOU truly were meant to be.

Comparing yourself to others takes away YOUR power.

Here's just a sample of the voices in my head:

- She's putting on a great event, why can't I?
- She wrote a book. Why is her story better than mine?
- She's such a great writer, why can't I write like that?
- She's getting these speaking engagements. Why can't I?
- Uh oh, another woman is putting on an empowering women's retreat. Why should I even bother?
- God, she's a great speaker. I'll never be able to motivate an audience like that.
- She's so funny! Why am I so boring?

- Of course, she can start a business. She's got a husband with a great job who is supporting the family, so she can just have fun playing around.
- Brené Brown has a book and a Netflix special, why not me? I'm an introvert. I understand research. I'm nice like her. (I never said my voices made any sense.)

All of this is nasty jealousy that's based in that pesky fear I mentioned earlier (Stupid Jack, hit the road already!). For me, it's the fear of not *being* enough and not *having* enough. If I can't be as successful as those women I'm comparing myself to, then I won't have enough to take care of my family.

It wasn't until I stopped trying to be what everyone else was, stopped comparing myself to others and realized I'm doing OK and not living on the street that the fear of not being enough went away.

For me, comparing myself to others becomes a vicious cycle: I want to be great like others, yet I want to be my own great self, but I don't feel like my own great self is enough, so I want to be great like others. WTF?

If you're comparing yourself to others, stop. I know, easier said than done. I did a lot of meditating and soul searching, as well as a lot of loving-kindness meditation, which I'll talk about that later in the book. I still compare myself to others, but now I catch it and that helps me stop.

What you need to embrace is that the world we live in is abundant.

If you ask yourself, "What makes what I'm saying or writing different than anyone else?" realize that you have a story to tell. Tell it however you want to, in whatever way calls to you. Writing, speaking, art — just stop comparing yourself to others. Tell your story. It may be the same story. But someone wants to hear YOU tell it.

There's plenty for everyone. If you need to compare, compare in a positive way:

- She wrote a book, which means there are women out there who will want to read my message, too! If she can write one and be successful, so can I.
- If her business is successful, that means mine can be, too.

- There's plenty to go around, the world is abundant. We can both rock this world!

Another one of my all-time favorite quotes is from Wayne Dyer:

"True nobility is not about being better than anyone else. True nobility is about being better than you used to be."

This single quote expresses the purpose of this book. It's why I have a crown on the "atta" on the book cover. It's why I'm wearing a crown in my picture.

When you're truly embracing who you are, when you love yourself for what you can do and stop worrying about what you can't do, when you stop comparing your journey to the journey of others, when you strive each day to love yourself a little more, that's your power, that's your true nobility. That power will help you share your gifts with the world.

There is no one like you. You do you. You ARE special.

You have something that no one else has. Find that. Love that. Share that. The world needs that!

If it makes you lots of money, great. If it doesn't, that's great, too.

What you will gain is a lot of peace and power from living the life you want.

When you dare to be you, the world answers your dare with a self-love that is like no other. You can feel that crown on your head.

Happy Act
Let's Go Crown Shopping

I want you to go shopping for a crown or tiara. I feel a crown is more powerful, but if a tiara speaks to you, that will work, too — after all, you can't spell Atta Girl! without a t-i-a-r-a!

Search online for "jeweled crown to buy" or something similar and purchase the crown that hits your heart, the one that symbolizes power.

Put it somewhere where you'll see it every day. I have a jeweled one that I keep on top of my computer screen. I look at it every day.

This passage from Marianne Williamson is one of my favorites, from her book *A Woman's Worth*:

> "What is a princess, and what is a queen? Why is the princess often a pejorative description of a certain type of woman, and the word queen hardly ever applied to women at all? A princess is a girl who knows that she will get there, who is on her way perhaps but is not yet there. She has power but she does not yet wield it responsibly. She is indulgent and frivolous. She cries but not yet noble tears. She stomps her feet and does not know how to contain her pain or use it creatively.
>
> "A queen is wise. She has earned her serenity, not having had it bestowed on her but having passed her tests. She has suffered and grown more beautiful because of it. She has proved she can hold her kingdom together. She has become its vision. She cares deeply about something bigger than herself. She rules with authentic power."
>
> —Marianne Williamson

Buy that crown. This is your symbol of nobility. The power that comes from just being you. Embrace it and wear it, even if it's just in your beautiful, powerful mind.

Atta girl!

 **ALERT!**

- If you catch yourself comparing yourself to others, stop and breathe. See if you can identify where it's coming from. Close your eyes and picture that crown on your head. Send those feelings (and your little friend, fear) off to the hills, away from your castle.

- The crown I have on my computer gives me additional feelings of power because when I purchased it, it came all bent in the mail. Not only did the company not pack it well for shipping, but it also didn't feel the need to replace it. So, I vowed never to do business with the company again, unbent the crown and donned it. I cherish the imperfections because they symbolize that no matter what comes my way, no matter how many dents form from others' crap, I'm still wearing that crown and no one better mess with me. (Don't you just love symbolism?!)

- Sometimes when you compare yourself to others, or try to stop comparing, you may think there's something wrong with you. There isn't!

- If you find yourself deep in jealousy or comparisons, embrace that with self-compassion. Every one of us has a shadow side. We're not perfect. When you embrace your shadow side, you bring in the light and love yourself more.

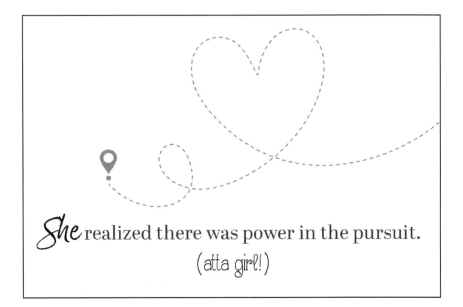

She realized there was power in the pursuit.

(atta girl!)

CHAPTER 12

GET RID OF THE ALL-OR-NOTHING MENTALITY

> "You can't be that kid standing at the top of the waterslide, overthinking it. You have to go down the chute."
> —Tina Fey

The sister to the why-don't-I-have-what-she-has mentality is the all-or-nothing mentality. (I know, quit with the sister analogy. But I have two older sisters, so I'm allowed to use the analogy twice.)

At the beginning of every Camp Atta Girl!, I suggest to the women to get rid of the all-or-nothing mentality. Many of us have the need to have whatever it is we're doing or working on be at 100 percent. That's great if you can do it. But quite often, it's not doable and it's tiring.

I tell the campers that even if they walk away with just one valuable piece of information, their day has been a success. There's no way, with all the information that I give at Camp Atta Girl!, for anyone to grasp it all in at once. That would be overwhelming.

Sometimes when women become overwhelmed, they stop everything. And when they stop everything, they end up with nothing.

Personally, this is a challenge. If I can't do it all, I either get frustrated or depressed — many times both.

Here's a sample of my all-or-nothing thoughts:

- If I can't run a 5K the entire way without walking, then what's the point.

- If I can't write a book that's close to perfect, why bother.
- I don't have time to clean out my closet, so it makes no sense to even start.
- If I can't lose five pounds a week, why start eating healthy?

Here's another example: While writing this book, a job opportunity came my way. I wasn't actively searching, but I discovered this job accidentally (Ha! Not really. There are no coincidences, right?). It was almost the perfect position for me. I struggled with what would happen if I took it. Would that mean that I'm giving up my dream of making a living on presenting "happiness" to clients? Would that mean I'm giving up Camp Atta Girl!?

In my mind, taking the job meant I had failed at owning a business. For a few days, I struggled with what to do.

But while my daughter and I were driving to dinner to celebrate her getting through the first week of school (we like to celebrate the little things), "get rid of the all-or-nothing take on life" went through my mind, and a big smile crossed my face.

I teach the women at my retreats to stop with the all-or-nothing, so why wasn't I practicing what I was preaching? I realized I can take a job and STILL do what makes my heart sing. Camp Atta Girl! is always a weekend retreat. There's not one reason why I can't do both.

As I stopped my all-or-nothing thinking around this issue, a peace settled on me. I felt so much happier.

Looking back, I think my all-or-nothing mentality originated in my childhood. I'm the youngest of three daughters. I think I often felt like I was supposed to be a boy, although my mom always said she was happy to have another girl. Maybe I overcompensated by being an overachiever. For example, when I was just sixteen years old, I oversaw the nightly closing of a department store and handled more than $30,000, which is around $125,000 today. What teen does this?

But all-or-nothing is exhausting. It's also depressing because if you can't do everything, you wind up doing nothing. You're at a standstill in life.

Life is filled with hundreds of wonderful colors; it's not all black or white.

When I stopped trying to have 100 percent and started being satisfied with doing ten percent or feeling grateful for what I had, life became easier and happier.

I think one of the reasons why I was struggling with my decision to take the job versus running my business fulltime was that I was also feeling a tremendous amount of sadness and guilt from spending so much of our family's savings on trying to follow a dream that didn't pan out.

One of my dear friends pointed out that the dreams don't end, they continue. I chose to follow my dreams instead of always wondering "what if." In her wonderful words, "There is power in your pursuit. Don't ever doubt that."

There *is* power in the pursuit. My pursuit doesn't end when I add something new to my life. I can pursue more than one thing. I also don't have to do everything at once to get where I want to go. There's tremendous power in that!

My ultimate goal for Camp Atta Girl! is to have 1-day camps in different cities and a three-to-four-day event held at a real camp, where women from all over the world come to have fun and find their inner power and voice. For now, I'm enjoying my job and loving helping women where and when I can over the weekends. It brings me such joy.

So, no matter where you are in your life, I encourage you to stop the all-or-nothing mentality.

- Want to do a 5K? Walk part of it. If you're in a wheelchair, wheel through it.
- Want to write a book? Do it. If you don't finish it, use what you have to write a blog.
- Want to lose weight? Don't worry about only losing three pounds a month. That's 36 pounds in one year! (Note, if you want to lose weight, read chapter 17. That's an order.)

Realize your own power of the pursuit. Start living and being grateful for what you can do and what you can have.

Atta girl!

Happy Act
J.O.T. It Down!

If you can't do what you really want to do just yet, write down a few things you can do towards it. Things that will make you a little happier until your dream is a reality.

I call it my "JOT It Down" list or my "Just One Thing It Down" — J.O.T. It Down — list.

Write one dream that you really want to happen:

_____

Now, what is **Just One Thing** you can do towards that dream? Doing just a little part of your dream will make you happier and energize you to achieve even more. No more exhausting all-or-nothing for you.

J.O.T. it down now. What's that one thing you can do?

_____

_____

_____

Copy the J.O.T. It Down template below and use this method every time you find yourself wondering why something isn't happening for you but is happening for others. Or, you can download it at lisabaileysullivan. com/happyacts. Use it when you find yourself doing nothing because you can't do everything.

Atta girl!

J.O.T. it Down!

This is one of my dreams:

_____

What is Just One Thing *I can do that's part of that dream, that will make me happier before I reach it? J.O.T it down!*
(atta girl!)

_____

_____

 **ALERT!**

- If you have a dream or an idea but haven't done anything active towards it, take a look at what's holding you back. See if you're tapping into that all-or-nothing mentality. Stop, take a breath and see if you can do a little of it at a time.

- Don't tell people your dreams. Well, some dreams you can. But sometimes, when we tell people our dreams, we focus on *having* to accomplish them. The pressure is on. Keep your dreams to yourself. This keeps your timetable between you and Spirit.
- Speaking of timetable, there isn't one. Whatever your dream is, it will happen when it's supposed to happen. Be patient.

She stopped trying to measure up
to everyone else's expections
and started measuring up to her own.

(atta girl!)

CHAPTER 13

CHASE YOUR SMILE

"As long as the ego runs your life, there are two ways of being unhappy. Not getting what you want. Getting what you want."
—Eckhart Tolle

Let's go back to college days and Psychology 101. Remember the ego? Ego is Latin for "I." It's the "I" or self in any person.

Here's a more technical definition: "The ego is the part of the psyche that experiences the outside world and reacts to it, coming between the primitive drives of the id and the demands of the social environment, represented by the superego."

Phooey.

The ego is simply this: it's your self-esteem, your self-importance and how you react to what people think about you.

In the previous chapters, I talked about how you need to stop caring what anyone thinks of you and stop comparing. You start to do this when you stop caring and giving attention to your ego.

Remember I mentioned my job opportunity?

I wasn't actively searching, but I noticed a job posted on Facebook regarding an opening for a communications coordinator for my town. I live in a small Texas town that's growing by leaps and bounds. It's one of the fastest-growing cities in the state and one of the fastest-growing small towns in the United States.

I love my little town. We lived here before, prior to us moving to Florida for my last corporate position. I love it so much that after I was laid off from that position, my family and I moved back, despite neither myself nor my husband having a job. (Talk about faith!) So, when I saw the town job posting, I couldn't help but look into it.

The communications coordinator position seemed to offer opportunities to both make a difference in my community and have a lot of fun. Plus, it would only be a ten-minute commute and was close to my daughter's school. Oh, and it would be nice to have some money coming in. (Starting a business as an introvert is *hard*. This may be my next book!)

So, I applied. During the initial interview, I quickly loved the job and the people. The job seemed perfect for me, but (gotta love the buts) ...

It was a coordinator position and paid only a fraction of what I had previously made as a corporate marketing executive.

Boy oh boy (girl oh girl?), did my ego rear its ugly head.

I wrestled with what people would think. I thought how in the world could I go from being a vice president of marketing of a national company to a communications coordinator of a small town. I felt like I was going backward, both in title and pay.

The thought of people thinking I failed in my business was spirit-crushing. My own thoughts of failure were spirit-crushing. The thought of giving up on Camp Atta Girl! was more than spirit-crushing, it broke my heart.

I wrestled and wrestled with what I would do if they offered me the job, and I became very depressed.

But when I took my ego out of it, I realized some key things:

- Who said I had to give up my business? I could work on it at night and on weekends. Camp Atta Girl! would live on!
- Why care what others think? The people who matter to me would understand and be behind me.
- If you forget the title and the pay, the position is a wonderful position.
- Maybe I'm changing direction for a reason. I'm a big believer in everything happening for a reason. So, maybe there's a reason for this.

- Maybe this position came into my life so I can make my *entire* city happier in some way! (I know, what a silly thought. But I believe in "big" asks to Spirit. If you want something, go big. Let your asks be bigger than your fears... much bigger!)
- I am not my job. That's not who I am. My job doesn't define me. My soul, my kindness, my love for my family and friends, my sense of humor, my love of beauty and nature, my love for myself and helping others — this is what defines me.

That last one is a big one. When you start believing that "things" are what define you, when you believe that who you are is what you "do" or what you "own," that's ego taking over. Who you are is not what you do. Who you are is not what you have. That's so far from the truth.

I started to realize how much of my life I've spent trying to prove myself to others, how much time I've spent judging myself, how much time I've spent telling myself, "That's not enough, what more can you do? How much more can you make?"

When I took ego out of this, I let go of this part of my story and started to rewrite it. I created a new narrative for my life. I let go of thoughts that no longer served me. I let go of the things that I'm not and embraced the things that I am.

While I was wrestling with my ego, I received a funny sign. I remembered a LinkedIn post about a woman who was following her dream but was embarrassed that she had to wait tables to bring in some money in the meantime. I kept thinking about that post, wishing I had saved it so I could go back and reread it.

The week before I started my new job, I was randomly looking through photos on my phone one day and noticed a saved screenshot of something. It was that post; I had saved it!

Remember what I said about signs? This was a big one. As I reread the post, tears rolled down my cheeks.

Brian Ratliff
Startup Veteran | Connector | Serial Networker | Director of Growth @ HiQo ...

Last week, I ran into a friend of mine who I hadn't seen in a decade. I was meeting a client at a cafe and she was waiting tables.

She left a management position at a big company last year where she made a great living to start her own business and needed to pick up a job that was flexible and would allow her to make ends meet.

At one point, she said, "I'm sorry you had to see me waiting tables."

It felt like a stomach punch thinking she thought I would look down on her for doing what she had to do to allow her to chase her dream.

My response was this:

"Don't ever apologize to anyone for chasing your smile."

It takes courage to chase happiness. You have to be brave to accept that your ego and pride may have to take a back seat until you're self sustainable.

You worry that your friends and family will judge you.

You're afraid you will pick up a former colleague when you grab a few Uber shifts to pay the mortgage.

You dread the thought of late electricity bill notices and credit card debt.

Most of us will never find the courage to get out of our own way.

For those of you who have and are chasing your smile, I salute you.

This was truly a sign. Things happen for a reason. No matter what happens in your life, stop worrying about what others think and "chase your smile."

When you follow what your spirit is telling you to do, when you follow what gives your life meaning instead of trying to prove yourself to others, your ego starts to fade away and you become happier and more at peace. You're doing things in life because they set your soul on fire, not because you're worried about proving yourself.

You start to make your life about meaning, not about stuff. You start living in the moment.

Stop giving ego the power.

Embrace all that you are, not all that you're not.

Keep chasing your smile, no matter what direction it leads you and take back your power.

Atta girl!

Happy Act
What's Really Important?!

Sometimes we let ego take over because we forget what is important in our lives. When you're trying to make a life-changing decision, simply write down what's important to you, what gives your life meaning, what makes you smile.

For example, here are a few things that are important to me, things that give my life meaning, in no particular order:

- Family, love, and happiness
- Helping my children become the best they can be
- Helping others
- Laughing and humor
- Treating people with respect
- Being a good parent and wife
- Helping my husband however I can
- Being creative
- Being real and authentic
- Being inspired and living in ways that would inspire others
- Spirituality
- Kindness and love
- Finding the good in things and people

Now it's your turn. **Find a quiet place and write down a few things that give your life meaning and are truly important to you.**

_____

_____

_____

_____

_____

_____

_____

_____

_____

_____

_____

This is not an overnight exercise. Come back to it. Keep adding.

When you're finished, put the list in a place you can look at often. By seeing what brings meaning into your life, you'll realize every day what is truly important.

Your job or title is not what gives your life meaning. Living to create a false picture of what success is will not bring you joy. What you do AT your job may be meaningful to you, but true meaning comes from within, from your heart and soul.

Focus on all that you are, on the inside.

Atta girl!

 **ALERT!**

- Once you start recognizing ego, it becomes easier to tell it to go away. But be prepared for it to come back when you least expect it. You can't totally get rid of your ego, but you can keep it in check. Be on the lookout. If you're feeling depressed or sad over something, maybe it's your ego.

- Regarding the previous point, I also want to make sure you know there is a difference between ego and standing up for yourself. If you are being treated in a way that doesn't sit well with you, don't just chalk it up to ego. You can keep your ego in check and still know when something isn't right, or someone isn't treating you kindly. It's okay to walk away.

- I'm not an advocate of taking a job that doesn't pay you what you're worth. For far too long, women have been underpaid compared to men. I know this firsthand. You deserve to be paid what the job should pay. There may be jobs that while they pay fairly, they pay less. These jobs may also touch your heart and make you happy when you walk in the door. You must weigh what is most important to you. Of course, what is important to you at age 30 is different than when you're 40, 50, 60, 70, 80 or 90.

- If you've started your own business and anyone talks to you about getting a "real" job, walk away. In the time I was laid off until I got the "real" job, I worked longer and harder than I ever have in my entire career. Since taking the job, I've worked even harder on my own business. Starting your own business *is* a real job.

- Accepting one thing doesn't mean you have to give up something else. You can always have a side hustle, or in my world and dancing, a side shuffle.

- Be on the alert for other people's egos, especially at work. If someone is being an absolute ass, that's his or her ego and insecurity coming through. Recognizing this will help you better deal with that person. Instead of anger, you may feel empathy. Having said that, some people are just asses. No empathy needed. Send them a silent "FU" and walk away. A big "Atta Girl!" for that!

- The path you're on is not the only path. Take a right or left turn if you need to.

STRONG

BRAVE

BEAUTIFUL

She only put the labels on her
she wanted to put on.

(atta girl!)

CHAPTER 14

GET RID OF THE LABELS!
THE POWER OF I AM

"Step out of the history that is holding you back. Step
into the new story you are willing to create."
—Oprah Winfrey

One of the ways to embrace your power, let ego go, and stop comparing
and caring what others think is to remove the negative labels people put
on you or you put on yourself.

These labels are everywhere: social media, magazines, television
and in your own mind.

You can find labels in the silliest of places.

I use a photo/image service in my work. For Camp Atta Girl!, I often
search for "woman dancing" or "woman having fun." I recently searched
for "woman thinking outside in nature" because I wanted a pensive shot
for something I was designing.

A series of women doing yoga poses came up. I clicked on the
images and was amazed at how differently they were described or
labeled: the first one was of a thin woman, the second was of a slightly
less-thin woman.

Young happy and beautiful red hair woman sitting on green field relaxed on grass practicing yoga balance and
acroyoga exercise outdoors smiling cheerful in wellness meditation and healthy lifestyle - Stock image ⋯

Overweight woman rising hands to the sky - Stock image ⋯

I know this is just a photo service, but it's a perfect example of the problem with labeling things. Here, women are described differently using weight-based labels.

Chances are that when you were growing up, you had labels placed on you, such as the smart one, the funny one, the pretty one, the creative one, the sensible one. Maybe you've heard people describe you as unhappy, angry, chip on her shoulder, too fat, too skinny, too old, too outgoing, too loud, too quiet. Maybe you're describing yourself that way.

Get rid of the negative labels you place on yourself or that others place on you. Only apply the labels YOU want on yourself.

Give yourself the power of I AM. (Remember this from Chapter 8?)

When I was wrestling with taking my job as a communications coordinator, I stopped focusing on what I am not and started focusing on what I am.

"I am" is powerful because what follows them leaves an imprint in your subconscious.

How many times have you said under your breath, "I am fat. I am having a bad hair day. I am depressed. I am unhappy. I am getting so old. I am so stupid. I am ugly."

Your subconscious mind hears those things and starts to believe them.

Embrace your power and who you are beyond the labels people put on you and start saying positive I AM statements about yourself.

Each time you catch yourself saying a negative "I am" statement, change it around:

- Change "I am fat" to "I am beautiful."
- Change "I am running out of money" to "I am abundant in every way."
- Change "I am so stupid" to "I am human and learning new ways to do things."
- Change "I am so old" to "I am still young. I am wise. I am healthy."

Turn around those negative "I AM" statements. The more you practice, the better.

At Camp Atta Girl!, we do a powerful label-burning ceremony and an intention ceremony.

We write down the labels others have put on us or the negative labels we've put on ourselves and we burn them. We release them. We let them go.

Then we write down who we are and what labels we want in their place: lovable, caring, inspiring, strong, bold, courageous and so on.

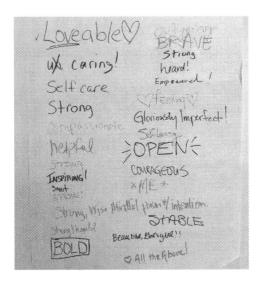

Whether you have your own label-burning ceremony or just do one in your mind, cleansing yourself of the negative labels is a powerful way to love yourself more.

We all have a reason for being here, we all have that inner light that was meant to be shared with the world. But if you're covered with negative labels, how can that light possibly shine through?

Get rid of those damn labels.

Atta girl!

Happy Act
Create a Burning Ceremony and Say Goodbye to Labels — Let that Sh*t Go!

A burning ceremony can be transformative. Through fire (a symbol of power, wisdom, and strength), you're more willing to let go of something that's taking away your happiness and no longer serving you. As you let go, you gain self-love for who you truly are.

So, let's create your own burning ceremony. You can do this with others or on your own.

Here's what you need:

- Paper
- Pen
- Lighter or matches
- A safe place to burn (glass bowl, firepit, fireplace, etc.)

Get a piece of paper and make two columns. **Think about the negative labels you and others put on yourself and write them down.**

Labels Others Put on Me: **Labels I Put on Myself:**

_____   _____

_____   _____

_____   _____

_____   _____

After you have compiled the negative labels, write down who you are at your core and want to be going forward. Write down powerful I AM statements: I am beautiful. I am abundant. I am grateful. I am me. Put a period (.) after each statement. Periods (all periods!) are powerful for women.

I AM:

_____

_____

_____

_____

Once you have the list, find an open area outside (unless you're using a fireplace) where the smoke will safely dissipate. Clear your head of any anger or irritation. Breathe deeply for a few moments. Feel at peace and grounded. If you wish, play a soft song in the background. I often use "There Is Only Love" by Karen Drucker, whose music I love. This song is particularly wonderful for this ceremony.

Once at peace, light the piece of paper on fire and place it in your bowl. As you watch it burn, take a few deep breaths and release your attachment to the labels. Think about who you are and the beautiful light inside you. Think of your intentions going forward.

Atta girl!

 **ALERT!**

- The next time someone says to you, "You're so <u>(insert statement here)</u>," decide right then and there whether to accept that label.
- If the label feels right to you, accept it into your heart.
- If it doesn't fit with who you are or who you want to be, smile and say to yourself, "That's not my label. I am (insert statement here)," and embrace it.

Realizing the energy of her words,
She spoke only magic to herself.

(atta girl!)

CHAPTER 15

THE POWER OF WORDS

"Watch your thoughts, they become your words; watch your
words, they become your actions; watch your actions, they
become your habits; watch your habits, they become your
character; watch your character, it becomes your destiny."
—Lao Tzu

The power of I AM is a shining example of the power of words.

Everything begins with a word.

Words create our reality. Without them, a thought or vision can
never be realized. Words are one of the most powerful tools in your
backpack.

Words have energy. They hold a vibration, they have power, they
give meaning, they inspire.

They can also do the opposite. Words have the power to impact us
both negatively and positively, depending on the words you use. So, it's
important to choose your words wisely and only pick the very best ones
to create your very best reality.

I have a deep love of words and quotes. Throughout my entire home,
I have quotes and words. Here are a few I'd like to share that are in my
office as I write this. Some are attributable, but most are just words and
quotes that speak to me:

- I am not afraid, I was made for this.
- Be who God made you to be and you will set the world on fire.

- Where God guides, he provides.
- Wake up, say a prayer and hustle.
- Life isn't about waiting for the storm to pass, it's about learning to dance in the rain.
- She is clothed in strength and dignity and laughs without fear of the future.
- By believing passionately in that which doesn't exist, you create it.
- Own it and bring it, but don't defend it or apologize for it.
- This is your year (btw, that's been on my computer for three years now)
- Be still for a moment, the world will wait.
- Laugh
- Live your life to the fullest now. Don't wait until you are an old woman.
- Imagine
- Believe
- Live
- Faith
- Be in the flow.
- I get paid well for being myself.
- I am abundant.
- I am grateful.
- I am me.
- Free spirit
- Your story matters.
- What can I do to love myself a little more today?
- And so the adventure begins.
- Wake up, relax, drink my coffee. (Oh, wait, that's on my to-do list I have printed and on my wall. It's an important "to-do.")

Whoa! These are just in my office. I didn't realize how many I have until now. I'm afraid to go check the rest of the house.

Yep! I believe in the power of words.

I've dragged my family into it, too.

Every New Year's Day, I "make" them choose one word that they will focus on for that year. (One of the many blessings about being a mom is torturing them with these kinds of projects.) I usually remind them of this "task" right after Christmas, so they can spend some quality time thinking about it — that's my hope, anyway. We also pick a family word.

Once they pick a word, then the real torture begins: We take a family photo to commemorate it.

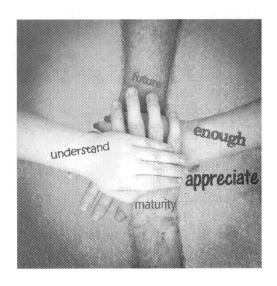

It's fun to involve your family when you start cultivating a love of powerful words, but it's not required. Start slowly with a few words or quotes that hit your soul. Write them down. Put them where you'll see them every day.

At the end of this chapter, I've included a list of positive words we use at Camp Atta Girl! See if you find one that touches your heart.

Here are some ideas to bring more positive words into your life:

Your Word of the Day
What would you like to focus on today or this week? Pick a word that inspires you from the list at the end of this chapter. Write it down on a piece of paper and put it in a prominent place.

Month of Inspiration

At the beginning of the month, look at the same list of words, select one and focus on that word for the rest of the month. Or, pick a word a day for 30 days and focus on a different word each day for a month.

A Year of Change

A powerful practice is to choose a word at the start of each year. Rather than focus on resolutions that go by the wayside, pick a word that you'd like to focus on for the entire year. Once you have your word for the year, display it in some way as a daily reminder, such as a hand-painted rock or something similar.

Family Words

Like my example above, together, choose a family word or saying to ring in the new year. Display it prominently for all to see daily. Also, encourage each family member to individually select a word to focus on for the year and write it down on a piece of paper.

Using Words at Work

Focusing on words is a great team-building exercise. At the kickoff of a department meeting or a project meeting, have employees pick a word for the week or month. Or, use some of the words listed at the end of this chapter to inspire you to create and communicate the core values of the company or department. Phooey to boring, long-worded mission statements that no one remembers. Choose powerful words instead. Work doesn't need to be stuffy all the time.

For Organizations

Have a board meeting coming up? Use the list of words as an icebreaker. During team collaborations, team building, and project launch meetings, this activity can help inspire employees to take the organization to the next level. Have the team vote on one word for the group.

Words have power. For example, a camper shared this after she practiced the power words for a month:

> "Following the retreat, I had some exciting opportunities present themselves, however, the familiar nagging gremlin of fear was also hanging around. My excitement about the opportunity to do something I was passionate about was often overshadowed by my mind creating 'what-if' scenarios that were less than ideal. I had anxiety and felt frozen even though the rational part of me viewed my fears as 'silly' and 'unsubstantiated.'

> "Lucky for me I remembered the onword & UPword deck from the retreat and decided to face my fears head-on. Each morning I randomly selected a word from the deck and used that as my mantra and focus of the day. As I drove, as I worked, as I found myself in uncomfortable situations I would think about the word of the day and the energy behind the word. As I purposely focused in this positive manner, I found the strength of my fears and the 'what-if' scenarios became less and less powerful. It was hard to believe that doing something so simple could have such a profound impact, but it did!"

Yep! Words do have power.

It's important to use words that inspire you. By using words that inspire, words that have powerful energy, you will change your thoughts, energy and your actions, which will bring more positive energy to you and those around you.

Atta girl!

Happy Act
On the Rocks!

You may have heard about or seen for yourself people spreading kindness in the world by leaving rocks painted with positive words or messages in random places for others to find.

It's not only a random act of kindness but also a low-cost and creative way to bring happiness to your own soul.

Here's how to do it.

- Go on a nature walk or hit a nearby beach to collect rocks (make sure this is permitted). Or, purchase some stones at a garden store or online.
- Grab your favorite art supplies to paint inspiring messages and words on them. If you're not an artist (although I'd argue we are all artists), the simple way to paint them is using paint markers, especially the ones that are specialized for painting rocks. You can find paint markers at any craft or office supply store or online.
- Look at the list of words included at the end of this chapter and select the words that speak to you and your heart, then start painting.
- The beauty of this is you do not have to be creative. Just painting the words and leaving the rocks around are enough to make someone's day. If you want to be creative, search for "painted rock ideas" online and oodles of painted rocks will be at your fingertips for inspiration.

The very first rock you paint should be one that hits your heart the most. This rock is the one you should keep on your desk or dresser to remind yourself of this word each day.

Remember: Words have energy and power. Choose words with special meaning, so when you see your rock, it inspires you to live up to that word every day.

Atta girl!

 **ALERT!**

- When creating word rocks, don't let any fear of not being creative enough get in your way. First, we're all creative. Second, all you need to do is write the word down. Think about it: If you discovered a rock that said "brave" on it, I bet you wouldn't notice anything but the power of that word.
- Don't want to paint? Go to Etsy or another personalization site and have your word put on a piece of jewelry or keyring.

up **Words**

Abundance
Accept difference
Achieve
Allow
Amaze
Appreciate
Ask
Aspire
Atta girl!
Atta boy!
Be
Be a friend
Be a little weird
Be a rebel
Be a unicorn
Be adventurous
Be authentic
Be charming
Be courageous
Be daring
Be fearless
Be fierce
Be gentle with yourself
Be happy
Be in the moment
Be patient with yourself
Be silly
Be spontaneous
Be the change
Be unique
Be wonder-full
Become the best you
Begin
Believe
Belly laugh
Blessed
Bloom
Breathe
Care for others
Challenge yourself
Cherish
Choose joy
Choose kindness
Collect moments, not things
Color outside the lines
Compliment yourself
Count your blessings
Courage
Create
Create a good life
Create good karma
Create healthy habits
Cultivate kindness
Dance
Dance in the rain
Dare
Decide
Determined
Discover
Disregard random negatives
Do everything with love
Do not judge
Do random acts of kindness
Don't be afraid
Don't give up
Don't stress

Dream
Dream big
Embrace change
Embrace the moment
Empower others
Enjoy
Enjoy the journey
Enjoy the moment
Experience life
Explore
Express gratitude
Express your feelings
Fall in love
Feel
Find the wonderful in today
Find your voice
Finish something
Follow your dreams
Forgive
Forgive freely
Giggle
Give
Give compliments
Give freely
Give hugs
Give it your all
Give thanks
Give your time
Good hearted
Grow continuously
Happiness
Hard is not impossible
Have a great attitude
Have an adventure
Have faith
Have integrity
Have no regrets
Have patience
Hope
Hug
I am
I am me
Ignore the haters
Imagine
Innovate
Inspire
Just believe
Keep on moving
Keep secrets
Keep smiling
Keep trying
Keep your promises
Kindness
Laugh
Laugh at yourself
Laugh freely
Laugh out loud
Learn something
Believe in yourself
Let go of blame
Listen well
Live minimally
Live with purpose
Live. Love. Laugh.
Look for opportunities
Love

Love fiercely
Love truly
Love unconditionally
Love yourself
Make
Make a wish
Make changes
Make good decisions
Make new friends
Make peace
Make positive changes
Make someone laugh
Make someone smile
Make work meaningful
Marvel
Miracles
Mistakes are lessons
Meditate
Motivate
Move
Never give up
No fear
Nothing is impossible
Nurture
Observe and listen
Observe the moment
Offer kind words
Open your heart
Pat yourself on the back
Patience
Permission to be human
Persistence
Perspective
Play big
Play with abandon
Practice self-compassion
Practice stillness
Pray
Purpose
Rebel
Relax
Release
Rest
Rise
Rise strong
See the good
See your own beauty
Seek excellence, not perfection
Seek wisdom
Serve with humility
Set goals
Share your ideas
Show up
Simplify
Sing loudly
Skip
Smile
Sparkle
Speak the truth
Speak up
Start
Stay curious
Stay humble
Stay positive
Stay real
Stay strong

Strength
Surrender
Take a chance
Take risks
Tell someone thank you
Think big
Touch hearts
Trust your instincts
Trust yourself
Try something new
Understand
Use your voice
Value truth
Win graciously
Wish on a star
Wish others well
Work hard
You are amazing
You are awesome
You are beautiful
You are brave
You are fabulous
You are kind
You can do it
You do you
You're special
You're the best
You got this

Laugh!

Let Go!

Dare!

Create!

Feel!

Rise!

Breathe!

Allow!

She realized the more she was grateful
for what she had,
the more she had to be grateful for.

(atta girl!)

CHAPTER 16

BECOME A BENEFIT FINDER

"A strong woman looks a challenge in the eye and gives it a wink."
—Gina Carey

Speaking of rocks, unless you've been living under one, you've probably heard about the importance of practicing gratitude.

There's been a tremendous amount of research done that clearly shows that expressing gratitude — writing down what you're grateful for — can increase your happiness. (I share more on this in the Happy Endings of this book.)

I'm one of those people who gets really irritated when someone tells me what to do. (It's not lost on me that I've written a book telling you what to do). So, writing down what I'm grateful for has been a struggle for me. It's not fun for me. It feels like a school assignment, and I've been out of school for, um, decades.

I do, however, love the design of many gratitude journals. If you slap a motivational quote on a notebook and/or design it in bright colors, I'll buy it. I sometimes buy them so I can gift them to others. But I love them so much, I rarely give them away.

If you looked in my home office, you'd find at least ten gratitude journals that have maybe four to five gratitude entries in them.

Clearly, writing down what I'm grateful for is not for me.

So, I've found other ways to help me express gratitude:

- I've embraced that it's okay to just express it when I feel like it.

- I have a large poster board on my wall and write what I'm grateful for whenever it hits me.
- I've created "happiness" jars, where I place notes of great daily moments.
- One November, I sent a letter a day to those I was grateful for.

But there's a practice that has helped me more than expressing gratitude: being a benefit finder. It's a powerful practice in which you find the "good" in something "bad" that has happened in your life.

For me, it's like gratitude on steroids. But it's not always easy. Sometimes it takes a while to find the benefit in the middle of a sh*tshow. The more you practice it (and it does take practice), the easier it gets.

When I got laid off, I immediately found the benefits in it. It just took a while for them to sink in.

- I realized I needed a break from working in the corporate world. The work didn't touch my heart and probably hadn't for a few years. I was a VP of marketing by day and a mystic by night. Being a mystic had become much more important to me.
- I discovered positive psychology. Ironically, if I hadn't been so unhappy and noticed others were also unhappy and stressed out, I never would have realized the importance of happiness in a company. I found that one of the things that made me light up was helping others find ways to become a little happier. Being laid off gave me the push to pursue something that touched my heart.
- I was able to create Camp Atta Girl! That's a biggie!
- I have met so many amazing women.
- I have written this book. Also a biggie!
- I am back living in the little town that I love.

No matter what difficulty you're experiencing, you can find at least <u>one</u> good thing in it.

In fact, the title of this book resulted from finding the benefit in a hurtful experience.

One way I promote Camp Atta Girl! is by sending out monthly

newsletters. I share tips on positive psychology so that my newsletters are useful, not just promotional. One newsletter centered on the importance of incorporating more fun into your life. (Research shows how important it is to do things that bring *you* pleasure.) I included a list of 30-plus ideas.

One of my newsletter subscribers replied back, "This is so bad. What kind of fun is this? Superficial, ridiculous and meaningfulness ... this is not creative, not fun and it would only give you pleasure if you are an idiot. Give me a break."

WTF? I can only imagine the expression on my face as I read this email.

Clearly, this woman misunderstood what my intention was. So, I reached out to her because I wanted her to see how unkind her email was and how she could have expressed her thoughts in a nicer way. The irony of all of this is that she was a fellow student in a past happiness course, so she should have known this.

After several emails, many of hers being similar to her first one, we ended up on common ground. She apologized for not understanding what I was attempting to do. It was a huge test for me to practice "not caring what anyone thinks of me" and to realize that whatever she was feeling was her stuff, not mine. But that wasn't the only benefit I found.

During my discussion with friends about how I should respond to her, one comment gave me the idea for the subtitle of this book.

> "Although we always have your back, this whole sh*tshow doesn't require it ... She is clueless and deeply unhappy ... I also believe that these negative people and ideas are very few. Just painfully obvious. I choose to turn my head toward the light givers."

Talk about finding benefits in the absurd! Because this woman responded so unkindly, I came up with the subtitle of this book. I'm grateful to her.

We all go through sh*tshows in our lives. And if you can still find your happy place in the middle of the sh*tshows in your life, then you are truly tapping into your power of not letting others take your happiness from you.

No matter what you're going through, you can almost always find a benefit at some point. When you do find that nugget, you're taking back your power to live the life you want.

Atta girl!

Happy Act
Practice Being a Benefit Finder!

Bad things will always happen. You can be happier, however, by finding something good in the bad. You can train yourself to be a benefit finder.

Let's try:

Write down something bad that happened to you recently. It doesn't have to be a horrible thing, just something you that you didn't like.

_____

Now, write down at least one good thing regarding the above. If you can think of more than one, great!

_____

_____

_____

Do this exercise for a week or more. You will begin to find the benefit in every situation. The more you focus on the good, the more positive you will become about life in general.

Atta girl!

ALERT!

- If you find yourself blindsided by something, don't react right away. Take a moment, step back and breathe.
- If you're blindsided by someone, not something, absolutely don't react right away. This is his or her stuff. This is his or her sh*tshow. Not yours. Stop. Walk away. See if you can find common ground, understanding, and compassion. It will help you find the benefit in it all. But if you can't, let that sh*t or sh*tshow go.
- I say you can "almost always" find the benefit in anything. I realize finding a benefit in some things may be extremely challenging. Maybe you cannot find one single good thing that came from a certain situation. That's okay. You usually can. Those times when you CAN find a benefit will help you during the times you cannot.

She realized the story of her life
was not quite finished yet.

(atta girl!)

CHAPTER 17

THE BISCOTTI PRINCIPLE

"You can't get to courage without walking through vulnerability."
—Brené Brown

Let's go for a walk.

This book would be incomplete without a chapter on my struggles with weight. While you may not have a weight problem (why is it called a "problem" by the way?), I would bet my Starbucks biscotti that you have struggled with your body image at some point in your life.

So, here I go.

I don't have a weight problem. My problem is I have let my weight define me for too long.

I am embarrassed by my weight. I feel ugly most of the time. I feel ashamed. I feel defeated. I feel like a failure. While I AM statements have helped, these feelings still come up at times.

For anyone who wants to contact me and offer suggestions on how to lose weight, I say this with love: F off. I've done it all. And don't get me started on thin people giving me advice on getting healthy and losing weight. *Grrr!*

Back to MY weight …

I could go on and on about where my struggles with weight and sense of shame came from.

The family trip to Puerto Rico when I was eight years old, where my most vivid memory is of my dad making fun of an overweight woman who looked like a relative, and my sisters laughing and chiming in.

Eating Weight Watchers meals in third grade.

Instead of my dad commending me in eighth grade for my first job delivering newspapers and my business savvy at such a young age, he told me how slim and great my legs look from all the bike riding delivering those newspapers. (I learned early on that looks are important.)

I can't count the number of times someone in my extended family has been on a diet or mentioned to me the diet du jour.

Yes, image was everything when I was growing up. Instead of thinking of myself as being smart or creative, I focused entirely on my weight. I was never thin enough. Even when I starved myself my first year in college (losing oodles of weight) and fainted in the shower from not eating, I still labeled myself fat.

I don't remember who put those labels in my mind. Maybe I did out of insecurity.

But it's funny what you DO remember in life. Someone can say what seems at the time to be just a random comment and you never forget it.

A random comment regarding my weight is one I haven't forgotten.

Around fifteen years ago, I was sitting outside with my oldest sister during a family reunion. I remember vividly when she said:

"Your story is your weight."

At the time, I thought that she was right. How great it would be to finally lose the weight, once and for all! Then my story could be how I lost weight. I could become a motivational speaker. My story could be a source of inspiration for other women.

Nope. That's not my story.

My story is finally understanding that I'm more than my weight.

I have been very successful at so many things in my life, including losing weight. I know how to do it. I just haven't been as successful at keeping the weight off. I've probably lost and gained around 500 pounds.

Around eight years ago, I lost 100 pounds and kept it off for a year. But then most of it started to creep back up from stress, worry, a new job and feeling unhappy. Starbucks biscottis were the death of me. I'd buy several and eat them in a day.

That craving for biscottis turned into what I lovingly now refer to as my Biscotti Principle: *Life is happening now. Don't let a biscotti keep you from living.*

Despite my shame over my weight, I decided that hiding behind it wasn't helping me. When you hide from anything, you lose your power.

Whether it's shame over your own struggle with weight or anything else, stop hiding from it and live your life – embrace your biscotti!

After being laid off, I stumbled upon (hmm) a profound piece of advice from Jessica Ortner, who does Tapping or EFT for weight loss (thetappingsolution.com).

"Take a deep breath and think about this. You are older than you've ever been before and younger than you'll ever be again. Life is happening right now. Imagine the horror of being so consumed with perfectionism and people-pleasing that you forget to live this fun, juicy life. Imagine rocking in a rocking chair and looking back, while thinking you never allowed yourself to buy that beautiful dress, go swimming in the ocean, even let yourself have a big belly laugh because of the circumference of your belly or the size of your thighs. **You never let yourself share your gifts that the world really, really needs because you were scared about what someone else, with their OWN insecurities, would think about you.** You look back one day and realize that you never really lived because you used your weight as a barrier you could hide behind. You spent years allowing your weight to define you. Like the saying goes … you are not fingernails, you have fingernails. You are not fat; you have some extra body fat. Having more or less doesn't define who you are, so don't let it be an excuse for shrinking from your power and denying yourself joy. Because the more powerful we feel, and the more joy we experience right now, the easier it is to create a beautiful life and to live that life inside a strong, vibrant body."

That hit me hard, especially the part in bold.

I was not going to be that woman rocking in a rocking chair and regretting not living a more fun, juicy life. If I had any gifts to share, I wanted to start sharing them. I wasn't going to hide anymore because I was scared about what someone else, with their OWN insecurities, would think about me.

I tapped into my power, ran to Starbucks to buy a biscotti (yes, I *know* "biscotto" is the singular form) and launched Camp Atta Girl!

My sister was right. My story is my weight. But my story is about not letting my weight define me. My story is that despite my weight and any shame I may feel, I'm pushing forward.

So, I'm writing this chapter to tell you that no matter what is holding you back, no matter what shame you are dealing with, listen to the words of Brené. Listen to the words of Jessica. Listen to the words of me, Lisa, who's been there.

- Do something right now that you've always been afraid to do.
- Go to that party no matter what you feel like.
- Put on that bathing suit and jump in the lake with your relatives.
- Wear that sleeveless shirt.
- Post that photo on social media of you in all your fabulous, real glory.
- Become trained as a Let Your Yoga Dance teacher and dance with joy and grace in front of all those skinny women and men.
- Embrace the fact that whatever you're hiding behind does not define you.

I'm not going to give you tips on losing weight. I never will. I believe my purpose in life is to give you tips on living the life you were born to live despite any weight issues you "think" you have or despite any other issues or shame that's keeping you from shining.

Because stepping out from behind your shame will help you take your power back. You'll feel a sense of empowerment you never thought you'd have. You'll love yourself in a way you never imagined. And you'll help others love themselves a little more, too.

If the weight falls off, great. If it doesn't, that's absolutely OK, too.

No more hiding. Change your story. Go buy that biscotti.
Atta girl!

(Whew! That was a long walk.)

p.s. I love the irony: My first name, maiden name and married name form the initials LBS, which, ironically, is the abbreviation for pounds. When deciding what name to use as a business owner, speaker and author, I considered replacing Bailey with my middle name, Ann. Ultimately, I decided to keep Bailey. If that LBS ever bothers me, I change it in my mind to Lisa Biscotti Sullivan. It's powerful to do whatever the F you want to do. Atta Lisa!

Happy Act
Whisper Sweet Nothings in YOUR Ear

This exercise may seem easy and yet it may be one of the most difficult ones in the book. It focuses on changing the way you talk to yourself.

I bet that you think at least one negative thought about yourself every day. More? They say it takes five positive things to combat one negative thing. Five. So, let's do the math: If you whisper five sour things in your ear, you should counter it with 25 sweet things.

But I believe that if you think one powerful, sweet thought about yourself — and *really* feel it — that one thought will drown out the dozens of negative ones.

So, pick a day you're going to work on your sweet nothings. The night before, **write down one wonderful thing about yourself that you truly believe:**

_____

If you struggle to think of one wonderful thing (something that puts a smile in your heart), ask someone close to you for her or his perspective. Write it down and post it on your bathroom mirror the night before. This way, when you wake up, you are reminded of that one good thing.

Now, for the rest of the day, try to catch yourself each time you think a bad thought about yourself. When you do, immediately repeat that one good thing.

Do this exercise at least once a month. You'll not only gain insight into how often you talk negatively to yourself, but also it will train yourself to say more positive things.

Talk to yourself like you would talk to a best friend or child. Why, oh why, would you say things to yourself that you wouldn't say to your best friend?

Whisper a sweet nothing into your ear. And then go grab a biscotti. Atta girl!

 **ALERT!**

- Beware of people who have never had a weight problem trying to give you advice. Toss a biscotti at them.
- If someone tells you that biscotti is Italian and is the plural of biscotto and there's no such word as biscottis, throw two biscotti(s) at them. I like the word biscotti and that's what I'm using. No shame.
- Don't eat a biscotti the night before you hold a Camp Atta Girl!, you might break a tooth. Been there, done that. (Luckily, it was a back tooth and they never knew.)
- I'm a believer in you doing whatever you want to do. If you want to lose weight, great. If you don't want to, great. But whatever you do, please, oh please, make sure you're doing it for YOU, not for someone else or out of shame over what others may think. (And you better live your full and juicy life before, during and after or I'll come find you.)
- It's never the weight. When I lost a lot of weight, I condemned my thinning hair, my wrinkles that showed more clearly and other silly things. It's never about the weight. It's what you think about the weight. Love yourself no matter what the scale says. (BTW, throw out the scale.)

- It may not be weight for you. Please, oh please, look past whatever "imperfection" you "think" you have. Take your power back! Live your juicy life!
- If you start worrying about what people say about your weight or any imperfection you may be obsessed with, find your best power song and crank it up. (It's "All About the Bass" by Meghan Trainor, "Roar" by Katy Perry or "F**kin' Perfect" by Pink come to mind. Check out the song list at the back of the book.)
- This may sound silly, but the following is a wonderful ritual the founder of Let Your Yoga Dance created: Walk around the room, saying out loud, "I love my belly, I love my butt." While saying this, alternate between tapping your hands on your belly and your butt. Trust me, it's very freeing!
- Go buy a biscotti. Atta girl!

She is mostly peace, love and sunshine,
mixed in with a little
What The F🪷☯️✌️?!

(atta girl!)

CHAPTER 18

THE POWER OF FORGIVENESS

"Forgiving is not forgetting. Forgiving is remembering without pain."
— Celia Cruz

As you know by now, I despise when someone asks me, "Are you happy?" *Grrr.*

Here's another one: "You need to forgive him (or her)." *Grrr!*

Injustice has always bothered me. Astrologists have told me I have three — not one, but three — past lifetimes where I was a spiritual warrior, fighting for causes and people. Not sure if that's true, but in this life, injustice ticks me off.

Forgiveness ranks right up there, too. I admit it: I hold grudges. If I think you've done me or someone I love an injustice, I will hold a grudge.

Yes, I know all the reasons why I should forgive. It robs me of my happiness and (insert sarcastic air quotes here) it's hurting me more than it's hurting them. But at this point in my life, I feel like if I forgive someone, the other person is benefiting, not me. Why should I give something to a person who has hurt me? *Grrr.*

But (deep breath) I also know forgiveness sets you free and is about you, not them.

It's just not that easy for me to forgive others. So, I'm taking baby steps.

Forgiveness doesn't mean you have to forget. It doesn't give people permission to still treat you like crap. It doesn't give them permission to do things that are still hurtful to you. And it certainly doesn't mean you have to become their best friend.

Forgiveness gives you a chance to step back and look at what kind of relationship you wish to have with this person going forward. Forgiveness means you can move on without them if you choose, that your happiness is more important than dwelling on what they did to you.

A perfect example for me is my relationship with my dad. He was an absent father for me. To the outside world, he was funny and the life of the party. To me, he was just absent. And honestly, I think I got angrier at the people who thought he was amazing than I did at my dad.

I tried my best through his last years to find some ground where I could connect with him. Sadly, it didn't happen. Talking to him was like talking to an elderly next-door neighbor.

While I was writing this book, he passed. My relationship with him was so absent that I had to ask my sister how old he was when he died.

Also, while I was writing this book, I was able to forgive him, just a little. A few weeks before he passed, he called me. As I would typically do, I ignored the call. He called me three times over the course of a few days. I ignored each call. (The best thing about iPhones is the caller ID – on a side note, FU robocalls.)

But on the fourth call, I felt that I should probably answer it. I'm happy I did. It was the first time in my life that I heard a true apology from him.

I was able to share a little of my feelings and truth with him, and in return, I received a true, sincere apology. He apologized for being absent, for not being the father he should have been. He apologized for a few other things, too.

I chose that day to forgive a little. It's a start. Baby steps.

And when it comes to forgiveness, that's all you need. Baby steps.

By taking baby steps, you will realize forgiveness is just the act of understanding the reasons behind what someone did.

I have a couple of tools that have helped me take baby steps on my path to forgiveness. One is to be "the watcher."

If you find yourself in the middle of an injustice or are feeling angry or resentful or if you just can't bring yourself to forgive someone yet, imagine yourself floating above the situation. Watch yourself and whatever you're going through. It's no longer you in the situation, but an actor in a play that you're observing.

When you're outside of the situation, emotions are taken out of it. You can view the situation with a clearer mind. It also allows you to be more compassionate with yourself as you work through the matter.

This method is not a new one. In meditation and many other spiritual practices, the act of being the watcher is well known. I use my watcher tool often — not just when working on forgiving others, but when my emotions are so tied to a situation that it's affecting my peace.

When you become the watcher, you begin to see both sides of the situation. Sometimes, you even see a comical aspect of the person who hurt you. You become an actor in that sh*tshow of hurt, and you realize that it doesn't affect you anymore.

Instead of being a victim of your thoughts and feelings, you are witnessing them go by. You get a sense of peace and release.

Here are some other helpful tools to help you take those baby steps:

- Give yourself permission to be human. Holding onto the hurt is a human experience and you're human. There's no good or bad about it. It just is. If you're not ready to forgive, that's OK. When it's time, you'll know.
- Don't care what anyone thinks of you. You're allowed to feel whatever the hell you want to feel.
- Practice gratitude. Be thankful for what the experience has taught you. See if you can find a benefit from whatever you're going through.
- Just breathe. Any feelings you're holding onto will go when it's time. There's no timeframe.

Quite often, what hurts and affects us an adult, is rooted in childhood. Often our feeling hurt comes from that little girl in us, that little girl who wasn't listened to and felt like she didn't matter. The same for those who have unintentionally hurt you. Sometimes it's their inner child who is lashing out, seeking love. Becoming the watcher helps bring out compassion for that person and yourself.

As you continue to take baby steps toward forgiveness, things will start to shift. The feeling of power over the situation will grow. Light will peek through the pain. You will feel more at peace and happier.

Atta girl!

Happy Act
Become the Watcher

Think of a person who has hurt you. Write down the person's name:

_____

Think about what this person has done to you and how it's made you feel:

_____

_____

_____

Now, close your eyes and picture yourself and this person. As you're doing so, visualize your spirit exiting your body and hovering over both of you. You are now the watcher of this situation. Send compassion to both of you and then bring your spirit back into your body.

With your eyes still closed, say aloud:

"The person I need to forgive is _____. I forgive you for _____."

Then, give yourself permission to be human and forgive yourself. Say aloud:

"I forgive myself for _____."

You can do this practice when someone has recently wronged you or if you've been angry with someone for some time. Do this daily for a week. It will help you begin to let go of the hurt.

Check out the loving-kindness meditation in Chapter 29. It's one of the best things you can do for your soul and happiness.

Atta girl!

 **ALERT!**

- Forgiveness is an important part of taking back your power and in giving you peace. I'm a total believer in forgiveness. But I also believe it must be on your time and terms. If you're not ready to forgive, that's okay. You have permission to be human.
- If someone gives you advice on the importance of forgiving others when you're not there yet, smile and go on with your great self.
- Forgiveness doesn't equal absolution.
- Most who have hurt you may not know any better. They are just trying to find their way in their world, and most have been hurt many times themselves. An example is my father. Knowing what he had to deal with when growing up helps me take baby steps. I just remind myself that he did pretty well considering what he lived through. But again, reread the third bullet.
- If you're working on forgiving someone in your family, like a parent, keep your interactions on social media to a minimum. In my opinion, social media can be deceiving, like everyone has a wonderful relationship with their parents. Every Father's Day or Mother's Day, the parade of "I love you dads" and "I love you moms" come out. If you grew up in a dysfunctional family — the ultimate sh*tshow — stay off social media during those days. Do something fun for yourself. Be your own mom or dad.
- If you must be on social media, keep an eye out for kindred spirits who may be silent or post about a spouse and ignore acknowledging a parent. Look for those like you and send them positive thoughts to help them get through the day, too.

She realized she was her own best friend.

(atta girl!)

CHAPTER 19

THE POWER OF FORGIVING YOURSELF

"Forgiving yourself, believing in yourself and choosing to love yourself are the best gifts one could receive."
—Brittany Burgunder

I think the greatest forgiveness you can give is to yourself. There's power in it. Even if you are just taking baby steps there, too.

If you are older than four years old, you know the importance of loving yourself. We hear it all the time! Social media is filled with encouraging "love yourself" quotations:

- "You need to love yourself."
- "You can't love someone else without loving yourself first."
- "Love yourself first and everything else falls in line."
- "Loving yourself starts with liking yourself, which starts with respecting yourself, which starts with thinking of yourself in positive ways."
- "If you don't love yourself, nobody else is going to love you." (How mean! I think this one deserves an "FU!")
- "Be gentle with yourself, learn to love yourself, to forgive yourself, for only as we have the right attitude toward ourselves can we have the right attitude towards others."

Ugh.

Loving yourself is hard. We've been ingrained to spend our days taking care of others more than ourselves.

Phooey.

If you don't love yourself right now, that's OK. It will come.

But you *do* need to forgive yourself. When you forgive yourself, the self-love grows.

- Forgive yourself for all the things you've said to yourself over the years.
- Forgive yourself if you haven't treated your body the way you "should" have treated it.
- Forgive yourself if you feel you haven't been the best friend to you or others.
- Forgive yourself if you feel like you've spent too much money on stuff you don't need.
- Forgive yourself if you feel like you could have been a better boss at work.
- Forgive yourself if you feel like you could have been a kinder person at work.
- Forgive yourself if you feel like you haven't been the best mom you could have been.
- Forgive yourself if you feel like you haven't been the best daughter you could be.
- Forgive yourself for all the energy you've wasted over the years not loving yourself.
- Forgive yourself for everything. All of it.

When you forgive yourself, you let go of the negative feelings in your life, like shame and anger, and you replace them with gratitude and power.

You let go of competing with and comparing yourself to others. Instead, you know that there's always enough. You accept yourself and all of your strengths *and* weaknesses. You feel more at peace.

Once you begin to forgive yourself, then show gratitude for the good you've done in your life. The more you acknowledge the good, the more your self-love will grow.

Don't try to love and forgive yourself all at once. Just try to connect with yourself more, so that you are your own best friend. Becoming your own best friend is a way of owning your power and acting from a place of kindness towards yourself.

At Camp Atta Girl!, we focus on what will help women lead better lives — self-love is a biggie.

As you become your own best friend, do things you'd do with your best friend.

- Take yourself to a movie.
- Take yourself to a restaurant.
- Take yourself to a spa.
- Take yourself on a nature walk.

While on any of these activities, go out on a limb and talk to yourself as if you're chatting with your best friend. It's okay to talk out loud, too. People may think you're nuts, but at least you and your best friend will have a great laugh over it.

Atta girl!

Happy Act
Do Just One Thing a Day

Sometimes the act of loving ourselves is challenging simply because we don't remember to focus on it. And when we do, we overthink it.

Loving yourself is simple. This tool to love yourself is simple, too. I borrowed this tool from Louise Hay, an author and founder of Hay House.

Write down on a piece of paper this question: What can I do to love myself a little more today?

Post this in one or more places where you will see it first thing in the morning. I have it taped to my bathroom mirror and at my desk.

Loving yourself doesn't take a monumental shift. It's one small act at a time.

Atta girl!

*What can I do
to love myself
a little more today?*

(atta girl!)

 ALERT!

- Catch yourself when you say negative things to yourself. Turn them around. For example, if you say, "I'm so fat," switch it to, "I'm doing the best I can and am grateful for_____," drawing on something about yourself that you DO like or love. (Remember those I AM statements from earlier.)
- Don't listen to negative talk about you. If your mom, sister or anyone makes a "suggestion" on how to lose weight, your hair color, how you cook or anything at all, smile at them and send them love and a silent "PHOOEY!" or "FU," too, if you'd like. That's their sh*t and insecurities coming out, not yours.
- Try loving-kindness meditation. You can find more about that in chapter 29.

THIRD ART

TAPPING INTO YOUR MOXIE

Moxie

noun

1: ENERGY, PEP — She woke up full of moxie.

2: COURAGE, THE DETERMINATION IT TAKES — She had the moxie to pull up roots and move across the country without a job, with a child in college, and a daughter in high school.

3: KNOW-HOW — They were impressed with her marketing moxie and hired her as a VP.

4: BOLDNESS, FEARLESSNESS, GRIT, SPUNK, ADVENTUROUSNESS — She spoke up when she wanted. She danced when people were watching. She had the moxie to start living the life she wanted to live, without giving a flip what anyone else thought.

(atta girl!)

Third Art: Tapping into Your Moxie

Distinctively Different

You know she's in there. That spirited little girl.
   She's original. She's quirky. She's unconventional.
   She's got moxie!
   She sees life as a wild and crazy playground.
   For far too long, she's been fenced in and told to be quiet.
   Enough!
   Let her out! Let her speak!
   Atta girl!

Happy Act
What Is Your Personal Brand? Who are you really?

Your personal brand is who you are, deep inside. She's been buried far too long and it's time to uncover her.
   Write down words that describe that little girl inside of you, the real you. Kind? Loud? Fun? Creative? Intelligent? Sassy? What words describe you? (Note: If they are truly describing you, your words will make you feel a sense of empowerment and peace and will make you smile when you read them.)

_____   _____   _____

_____   _____   _____

_____   _____   _____

_____   _____   _____

   Now copy these words onto a piece of paper and post them where you'll see them most often. It's time to start living with moxie.
   Or, take those words and create your own "elevator speech" on who you are.
   In the corporate world, an elevator speech is a "commercial" about you. It communicates who you are and how you can benefit a company

or organization. It's typically around 30 seconds, the time it takes people to ride an elevator from the top of a tall building to the bottom.

Create an elevator speech for yourself to repeat over and over. An example: I am a fun original, full of possibility and potential, full of compassion, kindness and moxie and making a difference in this world.

Atta girl!

 **ALERT!**

- When you speak your mind and your truth, show a little moxie. Be brave and fearless. People will sit up, take notice and listen.
- Moxie is VOICING that fearlessness. It's that wonderful feeling you get when you free yourself from the silence. Live out loud.
- Be aware: Some don't like moxie. That's their stuff. Don't quiet your voice because others have quieted theirs. Speak! Speak boldly.
- With great moxie comes great responsibility. The more courage and spunk you show, the more your world will change. Get ready!

She stepped so far out of her comfort zone
that she forgot her way back.

(atta girl!)

CHAPTER 20

STEP OUT OF YOUR COMFORT ZONE: MOXIE MAP

"Life always begins with one step outside of your comfort zone."
—Shannon L. Alder

It seems that as women's ages go up, their level of adventurousness goes down. Some other women, however, arrive at their "FU Fifties" or "Suck It Sixties" and are renewed and take no prisoners. The children are out of the house. There are fewer responsibilities. No more doing so much for so many. These women finally have the time to do things for themselves and don't plan to waste a single moment of it.

Whatever your age and wherever you are on the spunky spectrum, you can always get a little spunkier. You don't have to wait for your empty nest or fewer responsibilities.

Start your path to showing more moxie *now.*

The best way to do that is to step out of your comfort zone. Put yourself out there.

What is the one thing you've always wanted to do but haven't done — yet?

Get a tattoo? Learn belly dancing? Go skydiving? Take a long vacation by yourself? Write a book? (Wink, wink.)

Whatever it is, why haven't you done it?

What's holding you back?

For me, stepping out of my comfort zone was deciding to become a Let Your Yoga Dance teacher. I had never done yoga before. And in my mind, I was the opposite of what a person who teaches looks like.

But after being laid off, I felt I needed to do something I never dreamed I would do. Let Your Yoga Dance was that something.

I reached out to Megha Nancy Buttenheim, the woman who created the practice, and told her my fears. Her response:

> "I'm delighted to hear from you and believe me your question is a very common one. I think it's the most common of all: people worried about less flexibility or age or weight. I have everyone represented in my Let Your Yoga Dance world. People who are as old as 85 and as young as 18, people who live in very small and very large bodies, yoga and dance enthusiasts, and people who have been actual couch potatoes for quite some time, if not most of their lives.
>
> "Truly all are welcome in my training and some of my trainees who have lived in the largest bodies and have been the least flexible, become some of the greatest Let Your Yoga Dance instructors!!"

I signed up. Something in my gut told me I was supposed to do this. But despite Megha's beautiful answers and making me feel welcomed when I arrived the first day, I was beyond scared. I felt like a fish out of water. That evening, I sat on my bed with tears rolling down my face. I was so close to running out when the training had only begun.

Plus, I'm an introvert. Despite my many years of leading marketing teams and presenting to corporate leadership, I'm an introvert at heart. Doing this training was like sticking needles under my fingernails.

But I stuck it out. I showed some moxie and danced out of my comfort zone. After the first week-long training module, I came back for the second one and became certified.

If I had left after that first night, I never would have met Megha and so many other amazing women, whom I've had the honor of helping share their gifts with the world through my marketing experience.

If I hadn't taken that leap, I never would have created Camp Atta Girl! Let Your Yoga Dance is at the heart of my retreat for women. It's what makes the program unique and affects participants in such profound ways.

Finding your moxie doesn't happen overnight. You find it by facing the little scary things, one at a time, and by building up that fearlessness.

And it's building up that fearlessness that helps you face those sh*tshows you encounter.

For me, when I see sh*t coming my way, I now meet it head-on. This is why:

- If I can dance, in this body
- If I can help other women find their voice and power in this body
- If I can get up in front of a crowd of strangers and teach them happiness tools in this body
- Then I can handle any sh*t you're tossing my way in this body

And so can <u>you</u>.
Atta girl!

Happy Act
Let's Create Your Moxie Map!

Sometimes, all you need to start tapping into your moxie and getting the courage to step out of your comfort zone is having a game plan. I call it your Moxie Map. Let's create one!

Make a list of the things you've wanted to do in your life but have been too afraid.

Not ones that you haven't had time for, but ones that you haven't done out of fear.

_____   _____

_____   _____

_____   _____

_____   _____

Now, select one of those things and make a Moxie Map for how you can get there. As you travel to your destination, see how you can traverse those roadblocks.

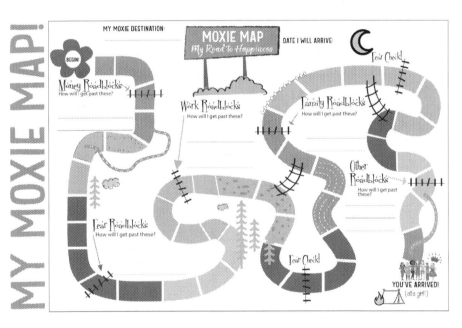

Roadblock: Money

Is it more money than you have right now? What are the ways you can generate what you need? Are there scholarships? Can you do odd jobs during your free time to make money?

_____

_____

Roadblock: Fear

Are you too scared? Can you identify where those fears come from? Is what you're fearful of true? (See Chapter 7 for Byron Katie's four questions.) Can you reach out to someone who's accomplished what you want to?

_____

_____

Roadblock: Work Commitments

Are your fulltime work commitments too much? How can you adjust your employer's needs to fit yours? Can what you plan to achieve benefit your current work? Can you show that to the company?

_____

_____

Roadblock: Family Commitments

Are your family commitments too much? How can you adjust everyone's needs to accommodate what you need to do?

_____

_____

Roadblocks: Other Things That Keep Me from Doing This

What other things are holding you back? Be honest with yourself. How can you conquer them?

_____

_____

Now, here's the really important part. Once you have figured out solutions to the obstacles, pick a date that you are going to do this one thing.

For me, I had a clear date for Let Your Yoga Dance training.

One of the keys to being happy is not just the journey, but having a goal and purpose, too. By picking a date, you are telling yourself this IS going to happen. You are making a commitment.

An important caveat on the date: Having a date is important, but if during your moxie road trip, you have to modify or push back your "arrival time," that's okay. Trust the Universe to get you there when you're supposed to get there. Having a date is important. Going with the flow is important, too.

Atta girl!

 **ALERT!**

- To me, showing moxie and the power of your voice are one and the same. It's time to use your voice to speak your truth, love yourself and your wonderful quirkiness.
- Bravely voice who you are whether someone wants to hear it or not. Use your outside voice. All. The. Time. (More on this in a couple of chapters.) I mean: ALL. THE. TIME.
- Be prepared for those who want to diminish your moxie and quiet your voice. Ignore those people.
- If someone tells you that you will never be able to do something because that idea is "too out there" or you're "dreaming too big," know that that's their stuff. Don't let them stop you from achieving what you want to achieve. Keep your moxie intact. I think it was Dolly Parton who said, "Would those who keep telling us it can't be done step aside for those of us who are doing it." I love Dolly.

Want to download a copy of the Moxie Map? Go to lisabailey sullivan.com/happyacts.

She realized it wasn't a gray hair...
it was a silver lining.

(atta girl!)

CHAPTER 21

YOU'RE. NOT. TOO. OLD.
Get to the Root of the Age Problem

"If you hear that little voice inside you whisper,
'You're too old,' shout back, 'You're an ASS!'"
—Lisa Bailey Sullivan

The older you get, the more moxie you should have. You've lived more, experienced more and have had it with the sh*tshows.

But for many women, having more moxie is not always the case. Some get older and quieter. Don't let that be you.

We hear a lot about FOMO: the fear of missing out. There's another one: ROOT. It's not referring to touching up the gray. It's about running out of time. Stop right now and tell yourself there's plenty of time. Seriously, tell yourself that — because there is.

I know that can be hard to believe, especially if you're a woman over 50. This feeling of "it's too late, I'm too old" is one of the biggest reasons why I started Camp Atta Girl! While the retreat is for women of all ages, I think it particularly speaks to women in their 40s and older.

There are images everywhere telling us how to age gracefully and be an ageless beauty.

Phooey to all this.

I spent the last years of my corporate life worrying if I was too old. It's not easy being an executive and hearing others say, "We need to hire more millennials" or "Let's start this employee board made up of employees under 35 so we can get their views and needs and wants" or

"Ooh, love that candidate. She will bring in fresh ideas." That last one implies that current employees are out of fresh ideas. Phooey, again!

When I turned 40, I felt depressed. Not because of the age, but because I could no longer be considered for those stupid "Amazing 40 People Under Forty" articles in trade magazines and newspapers.

Age discrimination absolutely exists, especially for women. It's a type of discrimination that's less obvious. There have been countless times I've witnessed women over 50 "retiring" or being laid off. You may have experienced this yourself.

While I'm a strong believer in fresh ideas and promoting diversity of all kinds, I think age is often excluded from the conversation. I applaud those in human resources who not only focus on diversity but also watch for age discrimination. (If you're on LinkedIn, follow Brigette Hyacinth. She has more than two million followers for a reason. She's a champion of how companies can benefit from hiring older candidates.)

While being laid off was a blessing in disguise, I've still had to do a lot of reprogramming around age. You can, too. Here are a couple of ways that may be helpful:

- Look at all the successful people in the world who started their success later in life. Search for "Successful People Who Started Late," and you'll find oodles of motivation. Further proof that things happen when they're supposed to happen.
- Change the way you celebrate birthdays. I'm 42 years old. Actually, I'm 58 as I write this book, but I decided that after turning 50, I would start subtracting the years. When I turned 51, I celebrated turning 49. When I turned 52, I celebrated turning 48, and so on. I wasn't doing this for the "wisdom" of that age, because no way would I want to go back to being 42 — I'm so much wiser and happier now when it comes to life. But I think it's helpful to have the mindset of being a younger "physical" age. For example, if I get an ache or pain, I think how would my 42-year-old self handle it?
- If there's something you've wanted to do, go for it! If it lights you up, do it. If it empowers you, act on it. Take the baby steps you need to get there. Because between now and dead, don't you

want to keep growing and giving back to the world? Use your Moxie Map to do it once and for all.

So, when you hear the little voice inside you tell you that you're too old to do something, drown it out with your louder voice.

Age is not holding you back. What <u>you</u> think about age is holding you back.

Things happen when they are supposed to happen. If God, Spirit, the Universe doesn't have a timetable, why do you?

There are a lot of people your age and older (and younger) who you can inspire and help. Start today.

Atta girl!

Happy Act
Forget the Time Limits, Baby Step by Step

Have you ever not started or finished something because you thought it wasn't 100 percent perfect? Besides worrying about being too old and not having enough time, sometimes we also worry far too much about perfection. You're left immobile. Baby steps can get you moving again. Complete the exercise below to identify what you still want to create and the baby steps to can take to get there.

What I Still Want to Create: Baby Steps I Can Take to Get There:

_____   _____

_____   _____

_____   _____

_____   _____

When we stop limiting ourselves with age, time and the need for perfection, we release the stress of finishing something and enjoy creating it. What would give you joy to work on and share with the world? Take those baby steps now. Don't be sorry tomorrow that you didn't start today. Change "one day" to "day one."

Atta girl!

 ALERT!

- It's never too late to be who you want to be and do what you want to do.
- Check out nexttribe.com, "the voice for smart bold women over 45." It's a lifestyle network filled with inspirational stories about women aging boldly.
- You're not growing older, you're growing BOLDER. Your moxie is on the rise! Along with nexttribe.com, check out growingbolder.com for inspiration. One of the founders was one of the good guys I worked with in my early career in television. He's still a good guy, helping everyone realize that life only gets better with age. Atta boy, Bill!
- If you're at work and see an emphasis being placed on hiring young people, speak up and remind them of the value of experience, too.
- If you hear anyone touting anti-aging, stick your cane up their ass! Embrace aging. Per the law of attraction, when you put "anti" in front of anything, you're giving it a bad connotation. Stop it. Just stop it.
- Think of your age this way: You're just coming late to the party. What happens when someone arrives late? All heads turn in her direction and she makes an entrance. So, throw open that door, strut your beautiful self into the room, announce that you *have* arrived and it's time to get the party started! Atta girl!

She used her outside voice. All. The. Time.

(atta girl!)

CHAPTER 22

USE YOUR OUTSIDE VOICE!!

> "For most of history, anonymous was a woman."
> —Virginia Woolf

There were two parts of the Let Your Yoga Dance practice that spoke to me the loudest: the solar plexus chakra and the throat chakra. During my life and career, I have felt like I lost my power and my voice.

My very first job out of college was as a news producer for a TV station. I was only 23 years old when I landed this job at an NBC affiliate in the top media market of Orlando. At the time, that was kind of unheard of for someone my age. But I had worked there as an intern the summer before and proven myself.

By 25, I was the producer of their No. 1 newscast. But it wasn't without its challenges. Before sexual harassment was ever really openly addressed and years before Gretchen Carlson took on Fox News, I found myself in a federal court filing a similar lawsuit against two of the news execs and NBC.

I won the lawsuit, but ironically, I lost my voice for many years.

While I felt immensely proud of having the courage to stand up for myself (still do!), being attacked by corporate men and lawyers took a huge toll on me and would for many years in my career. It was just my attorney and me up against their six attorneys and a bevy of powerful men. I can still recall that feeling of being attacked.

Throughout my entire career, I have had many great ideas, but I always questioned them. My voice always shook when I needed to voice an important point that I knew would be questioned and not agreed with.

I stuffed that anger of the situation and other similar situations deep inside.

So, when I was going through the Let Your Yoga Dance training and we focused on the solar plexus chakra and the throat chakra, it was like I struck oil. All of the pain and anger of losing my voice and my power from the past came spewing out in a wonderfully freeing way.

I knew that if I was feeling this, and this practice helped me the way it did, I should share it with other women. Camp Atta Girl! began to form in my mind.

I know from watching and listening to other women that these are some of the shared things we go through:

- We struggle to find words. We are afraid to speak up for fear of being challenged and not being able to answer that challenge.
- Our nerves surface when we try to speak up. Our voices start to shake.
- We believe we could be misunderstood (imagine a woman being misunderstood?!), so why bother expressing ourselves.
- We have a general dislike of conflict. So, we avoid anything that may lead to it.

If any of these things are affecting you, use your outside voice as often as you can. Speak your truth and express what you need to express.

Be loud and take up space. Your voice matters. Even if it shakes.

Here's why: If you don't, you aren't being your true self. Your voice is the embodiment of your true self.

In the words of Madonna: Express yourself!

If you cannot be your true self, you will never be truly happy.

If you cannot be your true self, you will never be able to set the world on fire like you were born to do.

Being your true self and using your voice reflects your courage, power, and moxie.

If you're afraid to speak up, it takes work. Here are some things that may help.

- Sing! Go to the "Music to Feel Your Power" song list in the back of this book, choose one and sing it loudly.
- Do karaoke. I know, the thought may send you into Starbucks to buy a biscotti. But imagine how you'll feel, standing at that mic, belting out a song and not giving a rat's ass what you sound like. It's freeing! And if you can't do it in public, buy your own karaoke machine.
- Write a letter expressing your thoughts. You don't have to send it. Putting your thoughts on paper is freeing.
- Have a dialogue with your fear. Remember at the beginning of this book, you named your fear. Have a conversation with her or him. Out loud, not in your head!
- Be honest. Speak from your heart, not to hurt, but with kindness toward whom you are being honest. But be honest.
- Do something creative! And if you don't think you're creative, that's when you should really do something creative. Express yourself through creativity.

And lastly, Dance! Pick out a song from the "Music to Feel Your Power" or "Music to Connect with Your Voice" lists at the end of this book and just dance! Dance like *EVERYONE'S* watching.

You do you. And express who you are to those around you.

USE YOUR OUTSIDE VOICE!! ATTA GIRL!

Happy Act
In the words of Madonna, "Strike a [Power] Pose!"

There was a past TED talk on power poses by a woman in the positive psychology field named Amy Cuddy. The YouTube video has netted an impressive 55,000,000 views. I recommend you watch it. She talks about how body language can make you feel more powerful and courageous. After all, look at how Wonder Woman stands. The epitome of moxie!

There's been a lot of controversy over Cuddy's research, many saying her claims were not true. Since then, she's come out and responded to all the naysayers.

I'm not going to get into all the research of what is true and what isn't. I do, however, suggest you read the amazing Forbes article by Kim Elsesser on the subject:

> "There is a substantial body of research that suggests that ambitious, successful women are not liked… And not only was Cuddy successful and powerful herself, but the goal of her research was to empower other women and minorities. If people generally don't like powerful women, we can only imagine what they think of powerful women trying to help other women become powerful."

I believe in power posing. It's worked for me. And if you need to find your voice in a situation facing or sh*tshow you're immersed in, I encourage you to strike a power pose. Here's how:

For the next week, each morning, take 30 seconds and channel your favorite superheroine. Before you walk out the door, take a Wonder Woman power pose:

- Stand with your hands on your hip
- Puff out your chest
- Tilt your chin up
- Hold it for 30 seconds

By commanding a power pose like this, you will feel more powerful and courageous and you'll be able to use your outside voice more often. Atta girl!

 **ALERT!**

- Sometimes, the research doesn't matter. The researchers I've ever worked would gasp at that statement. If research tells you one thing, but your gut is telling you another, sometimes you must follow your gut. If doing a power pose makes YOU feel more encouraged to use your voice, then do it. As Wayne Dyer says, "If prayer is talking to God, intuition is God speaking to you." Trust your gut. Do what feels right to <u>you</u>.

- USE YOUR OUTSIDE VOICE. I do believe the Rumi quote, "Listen to silence. It has so much to say." Sometimes silence speaks louder than words. Yes! But I also know women have been silenced too much. If you are one who is usually quiet, err on the side of making some noise.

- There will be people who don't want to hear what you have to say. SAY IT ANYWAY.

She finally realized what they meant when they said, "F 'em if they can't take a joke."

And she lived happily ever after.

(atta girl!)

CHAPTER 23

DON'T FORGET TO LAUGH!

"Laugh. Laugh as much as you can. Laugh until you cry. Cry until you laugh. Keep doing it even if people are passing you on the street saying, 'I can't tell if that person is laughing or crying, but either way they seem crazy, let's walk faster.'"
—Ellen DeGeneres

Does it feel like you sitting through more and more sh*tshows? That's probably because there is an epidemic of seriousness in our world today.

If you do nothing in the middle of a sh*tshow, for the love of God, laugh.

Laughter and humor can get you through anything.

Mayo Clinic research proves it's also good for you. When you laugh, it doesn't just lighten your mental load, it also induces physical changes in your body. Laughter enhances your intake of oxygen-rich air, stimulates your heart, lungs, and muscles, and it increases the endorphins that are released by your brain.

Research aside, it's cathartic.

I can't tell you how many times laughter and humor have helped me get through sh*tshows, especially at work. ("The Office" was such a popular sitcom with good reason.)

Every single place I've worked at, there's been one person I could go to for a good laugh.

At my first job at the TV station, which I mentioned in a previous chapter, it was Bart. As I experienced the working world sh*tshow and all its challenges, Bart always helped me find something to laugh at. He kept me laughing so much that I ended up marrying him. And he's kept me laughing ever since. Not only do I think he's the funniest person I've ever known, he's also the kindest. It's like having my own version of Ellen DeGeneres.

When I worked for a commercial fishing company (yep, my first marketing job was marketing dead fish), it was Dawn. She'd make me laugh no matter what was happening.

At my first newspaper job, it was Rich. People used to say I was the Ed McMahon to his Johnny Carson.

At my second newspaper job, it was Kathy. She would get me wheezing by sending me a funny photo or a one-liner, just at the right time. Sometimes, we would laugh so hard together we couldn't breathe.

At my last corporate job, before being laid off, it was Chuck, who understood my sense of humor. Through his humor and our shared laughter, it helped reassure me I wasn't going nuts. (Well, not totally.)

And then when I was laid off from that job and going through the sh*tshow that followed, Bart was there to keep me laughing and keep me going.

Whether at work or in life, the key to getting the most out of laughter and humor is to make sure you find someone who gets your sense of humor. For example, you're reading this book because the title, which might offend some, spoke to you and made you laugh. We get each other! Atta girls! (I do believe, however, that "sh*tshow" resonates with a lot of people because it's a funny way to describe a hellish situation.)

Later, I will discuss internal or character strengths. These are the positive qualities that come naturally to you. They affect the way you think, feel and behave in all aspects of your life. Character strengths are viewed as "who we are." They are part of our core identity.

Humor is one of my top internal strengths. It doesn't necessarily mean I'm funny, it means I like to laugh, and I try to bring a lighter side into gloomy situations. (Ta da! Thus, the reason for this book. And it only took 23 chapters to get to the core reason.)

I believe humor can make the intolerable more bearable and the ordinary more fun. I believe humor can help bring relief to your suffering and can put you at ease in stressful situations. Have you noticed how the energy shifts in stressful meetings when someone makes a joke?

Ahead of each Camp Atta Girl! retreat or corporate session to help employees cultivate more happiness on the job, I have each participant take a survey to identify their top inner strengths. Every now and then, I find people who have humor as their lowest strength. Because humor is particularly important to me, I sometimes seek them out to see how we can add more humor into their lives.

Wondering where humor falls in your life? In the upcoming chapter on character strengths, I'll show you how you can identify what yours are.

Whether humor and laughter are among your top strengths or not, find that one person who makes you laugh. Heck, find several people who make you laugh. The more, the merrier.

Plus, when you're happier, so is this world we live in.

Atta girl!

Happy Act
Have a Laughter Day

It's easy to take life seriously, especially when serious things are happening all around us. But it can't be all doom and gloom. It's important that you bring more laughter and humor into your life, especially if you're going through a sh*tshow. Here's how:

- Make laughing part of your morning ritual with a joke-of-the-day calendar or by reading a funny daily quote.
- Hang out with funny people. (This is a must!)
- Watch YouTube videos of your favorite comedian. (My favorite: George Carlin.)
- Watch funny TV shows.
- Go to a funny movie.
- Eat a bag of Laffy Taffy and read the jokes on the wrappers.
- Go to a comedy club.
- Read humorous books.
- Take a Laughter Yoga class.

- Ask Alexa to make you laugh. Also, ask Alexa to tell you you're awesome.
- Start a Pinterest board of funny stuff.
- Put laughter quotes on your walls.
- Follow funny people on Twitter, Facebook, and Instagram.
- Unfollow people on Twitter, Facebook, and Instagram who bring you down.
- Start a work or home Joke Jar. Read one or more each Friday.
- Listen to funny podcasts.

Let's make a list of things that make <u>you</u> laugh:

_____ _____ _____

_____ _____ _____

_____ _____ _____

_____ _____ _____

Now, pick a day that you can dedicate to nothing but laughter and humor — I'm serious! If you can't pick an entire day, set aside a few hours.

Play a couple of movies that make you laugh. Read something that makes you laugh. Hang out with your partner, child or grandchild and enjoy lots of laughs. Schedule a girls-day-out with the friend that makes you laugh the most.

Focus on nothing but laughing and humor.

Atta girl!

 ALERT!

- For the love of God, if you have a boss who doesn't make you laugh, doesn't understand your humor or anyone's humor, or who doesn't believe the value of laughter at your company, run for the hills!

- Seek out those who make you laugh, in life and at work. While there was always one main person I could go to at work to make me laugh, truth is that everywhere I worked, I had several I could go to. Find your sidekick in humor wherever you go.
- Be careful not to let your humor hurt or bully others. Humor at another person's expense is not humor. But you knew that.
- Remember: permission to be human. It's okay to feel all the feels. If you don't feel like laughing, that's okay. But when you can, do try. You'll feel better.
- Give yourself permission to be silly or a whack-a-doodle (love those words!). Laugh at yourself. Don't take yourself too seriously.
- It's possible that laughing can burn the same number of calories as six to ten minutes on a treadmill. So, go ahead and laugh your ass off. Atta girl!

She was a little too out
there for most people.

(atta girl!)

CHAPTER 24

DANCE LIKE EVERYONE'S WATCHING: INTRODUCING LET YOUR YOGA DANCE®

"To live is to dance... to dance is to live!"
—Snoopy

One way to feel bolder, more fearless and happier (and filled with moxie) in the middle of a sh*tshow is to give yourself permission to dance.

Research shows that dancing reduces anxiety, activates the brain's pleasure circuits, improves body image, helps combat dementia and more. That aside, it's just plain old fun to let yourself and your cares go, like when you were a child.

Think back to when you were around five or six years old. You might have been one of those little girls who couldn't wait to start dance classes. Remember the fun you had each week? Remember how you felt putting on the brightly colored sequined costume or tutu for your first recital? Maybe you could care less about what you wore, and it was all about busting a move in class or at home.

Where did that little girl go?

She's still there.

For many of us, we've grown into women who feel tense and awkward in our bodies. So, instead of enjoying dancing, we focus on not having that perfect body and worry about what people may think. Instead of feeling the music, we're feeling their eyes on us.

The ultimate form of tapping into your power and living fearlessly happy is dancing like *everyone's*, not just no one's, watching. It's the epitome of having moxie. If you can let go of those fears, dance freely and enjoy yourself, it can change your life.

That's why dancing is the most important component of Camp Atta Girl!

And the best dancing of all? Let Your Yoga Dance. I'll talk more about this practice in the next chapter, but I want to point out one word in this practice: Note that it's called Let <u>Your</u> Yoga Dance.

One of the reasons why I fell in love with this practice is because of that one word. I realized that I was playing small and hiding. For a long time, I was waiting for when I was thin enough (phooey!) to play big. I cared more about what others thought of me than what was right for me. Let Your Yoga Dance helped me to discover that one of the ways I could find more happiness was for me to just be me.

So, turn on the music and dance YOUR dance like *everyone's* watching.

Happy Act
Care to Dance?

If you can, find a Let Your Yoga Dance class in your area and attend. If one isn't available, turn to the end of Chapter 25 for specific songs that can help you connect on your own with the different energy centers within you. Choose a song that fits with how you are feeling or *want* to feel and simply move your spirit to the song.

What's most important is that you dance — however and whenever you want to.

Atta girl!

P.S. If you want to tap into your moxie even deeper and help others do the same, consider going through Let Your Yoga Dance teacher training. If I can do it, anybody and any "body" can do it. Go to letyouryogadance.com.

ALERT!

- Don't let your mind play tricks on you or let your ego get the better of you. It's not about how you think you look dancing. It's about how you feel!
- Worried about your body image dancing? Be like Lizzo. (Google her!)
- If you can, incorporate movement into your work or company. I used to kick off my weekly department meetings by loudly playing a song-of-the-week to get the spirits up in my department, hoping everyone would get up and dance. Most of the time, I was the only one moving. If that's you, don't let it stop you. Keep right on dancing! Adding positive energy to a department is just as important as the work that's being done.
- Snoopy is right.

FOURTH ART

HAPPY ~~ENDINGS~~

BEGINNINGS

Beginnings

noun

1: POINT IN TIME WHERE OR SPACE AT WHICH SOMETHING BEGINS — She started her new journey at the beginning of 2020.

2: THE FIRST PART OR EARLIEST STAGE OF SOMETHING — She left her current situation and finally started living her life.

3: THE BACKGROUND OR ORIGINS OF ANYTHING — She rose from the challenges and took on the world.

4: THE START OF SOMETHING FABULOUS — She changed her thoughts about what life was supposed to be, advanced confidently in the direction of her dreams, and lived the happier life she had imagined.

(atta girl!)

Happy ~~Endings~~ Beginnings

Happier Ever After

Throughout this book, I've shared tips and tools that have helped me tap into my power and moxie and live fearlessly happy. Some are based in science, backed by research; and some are based in woo-woo, supported by the personal experiences of millions of people.

Remember, I describe this book as a carefully curated ensemble of the science and the woo-woo.

In this section, I offer more of the science. I offer some positive psychology tools that can help you tap into your happiness. After all, we started with happiness, so we should end with it. Take what works for you!

These are some of the same tools that I teach and share at Camp Atta Girl! and at the workshops I hold for companies, schools, and organizations. There are many tools, these are some of my favorites.

Remember, no one is happy all the time. But these tools will help you become happier throughout your life.

If you'd like to learn more about the science and research behind positive psychology, I encourage you to check out some of the resources I include at the end of this book and also search online for the many books and articles available on this topic.

I hope that these tools help you create a more fulfilling life. May they help you be the woman you were always meant to be.

There are no endings … just happy beginnings.

Atta girl!

She knows she'll eventually get to
where she wants to be.

But damn, she's gonna have fun and dance,
dance, dance along the way."

(atta girl!)

CHAPTER 25

LET'S GET PHYSICAL: MORE ON
LET YOUR YOGA DANCE®

"You are a dancer. Even if you've been a couch potato, are a
computer geek, or have been physically challenged your entire
life, you're still a dancer. You may not be a professional dancer,
but you're a dancer, nonetheless. It's your birthright."
—Megha Nancy Buttenheim

For a full year, I studied with the Wholebeing Institute, where I
immersed myself in the science of happiness and became certified in
positive psychology.

One of the tenets of positive psychology that I learned during my
certification is the happiness model. The essence of this model is that
happiness can be found by focusing on SPIRE — spiritual, physical,
intellectual, relational and emotional well-being.

I would like to focus on the "P" — the physical.

When some women hear the word "physical," their brains go numb.
They think it means a lot of work, but it doesn't have to be. It can

be wonderful and fun, which is exactly what Let Your Yoga Dance embodies.

If women hesitate to sign up for Camp Atta Girl!, it's usually because they're a little shy about the movement and dance part of it. I understand. At first, I couldn't picture myself sashaying across a dance floor because I thought I was too out of shape and not a skinny-mini.

But when I was laid off, Let Your Yoga Dance brought joy back into my spirit. It helped me get through the sh*tshow.

What Exactly *Is* Let Your Yoga Dance?

Created by the amazing Megha Nancy Buttenheim, it is a beautiful practice for all shapes, sizes, and ages that uses expressive movements to lift your spirit, invoke joy and help you tap into your real and authentic self. It combines yoga, the breath, user-friendly movement, and dance and fabulous music from around the world. Each song and dance connect to a specific energy center/chakra of your body.

Working through the rainbow of colors, you begin with red, feeling safe and grounded and connected to the earth, and you travel through to violet, feeling connected to Spirit.

As I mentioned in the previous chapter, I encourage you to look for a class in your area at letyouryogadance.com. If you cannot find one, check out the following music lists for songs that match what you want to work on — from your power and voice to self-love. Or, if you already have a list of go-to tunes that deeply touch your spirit, great!

Whatever the song, crank it up, get physical and DANCE!

Atta Girl!

Music For Connecting with Safety
Grounding. Strength. Roots. Safety.

This music and movement connects to the Earth, to the feet, legs, and tailbone. So many women are up in their heads, worrying. Women want to feel grounded, safe and it all starts with the foundation. This music connects you to Earth, the best foundation of all.

SONG	ARTIST
Be The Change	MC Yogi
Bolero	Ravel
Circle of Life	Lion King Soundtrack
Ganapati Om	Donna De Lory
Hari Om	Miten
In Beauty May I Walk	Karen Drucker
Loka	Ena Vie
Ong So Hung	Guru Singh
Relaxation	Deep Forest
Storms in Africa	Enya
Summer Breeze	Seals & Croft
The Bare Necessities	From Jungle Book
The Calling	Santana feat. Eric Clapton
The Calling	Shawn Galloway
Today I Choose	Karen Drucker
Under the Sea	Samuel E. Wright

Slow
Rhythmical

I Am Safe.

Enlivening

Music For Loving Yourself
Self-Love. Relationships. Your Purpose.

This music and movement taps your heart and is all about compassion, Love, self-love and kindness. A woman's greatest power is self-love.

SONG	ARTIST
All you need is Love	Beatles
Baby Love	Supremes
Believe	Cher
Blessing to the World	Karen Drucker
Build Me Up Buttercup	The Foundations
Crazy Little Thing Called Love	Queen
Dancing	Kylie Minogue
Defying Gravity	Idina Menzel
Everybody	Ingrid Michaelson
Express Yourself	Madonna
Fallin'	Alicia Keys
Good Feeling	Flo Rida
Have it all	Jason Mraz
Hold on Forever	Rob Thomas
I Choose Love	Shawn Galloway
I Need to Know	March Anthony
I'm so Grateful	Karen Drucker
I Say a Little Prayer	Aretha Franklin
Just the Way you Are	Glee Cast
Love Shack	The B 52's
Love Train	The O Jays
Love You Like a Love Song	Selena Gomez
Rainbow Connection	Sarah McLachlan
There is Only Love	Karen Drucker
Viva La Vida	Cold Play
What the world needs now	Union of Sound
You're the one that I want	Olivia Newton John /John Travolta

Upbeat love

Energetic

I Am Love.

Music to Feel Your Power
Power. Strength. Self-esteem. Warrior

This music and movement helps you tap into your power. Turn on the drums and think fire. Turn on Katy Perry and roar. Dance and sing your power and authority. You are strong and brave. You can stand strong even when terrified, and move forward anyway.

SONG	ARTIST
Applause	Lady Gaga
Batakatu	KDZ The Drummers of Kripalu Live
Brave	Sara Bareillas
Disco Inferno	The Trammps
Everybody Dance Now	C+C Music Factory
Fight Song	Rachel Platten
Fxxxkin Perfect	Pink
Get this party started	Pink
Good Morning (feat. TobyMac)	Mandisa
Hit me with your best shot	Pat Benetar
I got a feeling	Black Eyed Peas
In this World	Moby
Invincible	Kelly Clarkson
Like it or Not	Madonna
Man! I Feel Like a Woman!	Shania Twain
Me Too	Meghan Trainor
N-O is my New Yes	Karen Drucker
Respect	Aretha Franklin
Roar	Katy Perry
Send in the Drums	James Asher
Sexy Back	Justin Timberlake
Shake it Off	Taylor Swift
She	Promilla
Single Ladies (Put a Ring On It!)	Beyonce
Soak Up the Sun	Sheryl Crow
Strength, Courage, Wisdom	India Arie
Survivor	Destiny s Child
Unlabeled	Isabelle
What Doesn't Kill You (Stronger)	Kelly Clarkson
That's Not My Name	The Ting Tings
This One's For the Girls	Martina McBride
Uptown Funk	Mark Ronson
Walk this Way	Aerosmith
We Got the Beat	The Go Go's

POWER SONGS

Feel the beat

Brave

Drums

I Am Strong.
I AM Powerful.

Music to Connect with Your Voice
Self-expression. Communication. Authenticity.

This music represents sound, truth. When you use your voice, you are wild and free. Sometimes women are afraid to express themselves. Don't be! Be your authentic self, not afraid to sing out loudly, dance amd express yourself. This music is similar to Power, because Voice and Power are so connected - using your voice, gives you Power. Feeling Powerful, gives you the courage to be you! Play any music that fills your body, heart, and brain with freedom of expression! Be wild, be fun, be you!

SONG	ARTIST
All She Wants to Do	Don Henley
All That Jazz	Catherine Zeta Jones
America's Sweetheart	Ellie King
Born This Way	Lady GaGa
Can't Stop the Feeling	Justin Timberlake
Crocodlie Rock	Elton John
Dance to the Music	will.i.am
Dancing in the Dark	Bruce Springsteen
Firework	Katy Perry
Footloose	Kenny Loggins
Get this Party Started	Pink
Girls Just Want to have Fun	Cindy Lauper
Go Out Dancing	Kylie Minogue
Hand Clap	Fitz and the Tantrums
Happy	Pharrel Williams
I Don't Care	Judy Garland
I Don't Have to Be Perfect	Karen Drucker
Joyful Sound	Debby Holiday
Just Dance	Lady GaGa
New Attitude	Patti LaBelle
On Top of the World	magine Dragons
Shut up and Dance	Walk the Moon
Some Days You Gotta Dance	Dixie Chicks
SOS	Rihanna
That's Not My Name	The Ting Tings
Uptown Funk	Mark Ronson
Vogue	Madonna
Walking on Sunshine	Katrina & the Waves
Wake Me Up Before you Go-go	Wham!

MOXIE SONGS

Fun!

Wild!

Free!

I Speak.
I Am Expressive.

Music For Acceptance
Creativity. Pleasure. Emotions.

This music and movement connects to water, fluidity, creativity, body love and acceptance. Sway your hips and love your beautiful self!

SONG	ARTIST
All About the Bass	Meghan Trainor
Black Magic Woman	Santana
Female	Keith Urban
Fever	Eva Cassidy
Love	Mary J. Blige
Smooth	Santana
Sweet Love	Trisha Yearwood
S'Wonderful	Diana Krall
Wade in the Water	Eva Cassidy
You Gotta Move	Sam Cooke

Bluesy *Fluid*

I Am Creative.

Watery

Music For Imagining
Intuition. Self-Reflection. Clarity.

This music connects to light, intuition, and clear seeing. Let your soul sing for joy. Let your female spirit connect with your vision and purpose.

SONG	ARTIST
A Thousand Years	Christina Perri
A Woman Feels Her Power	Karen Drucker
Amazing Grace	Cecelia
Angel	Sarah McLachlan
Earth Prayer	Ena Vie
Greatest Love of All	Whitney Houston
He Ma Durga	Donna DeLory
How Could Anyone	Shaina Noll
Human	Christina Perri
I Am Beautiful	Karen Drucker
I Am Light	India Arie
I Am So Blessed	Karen Drucker
I Believe	Cecilia
I Hope You Dance	Lee Ann Womack
Imagine	Eva Cassidy
Let it Be	The Beatles
Let There Be Peace on Earth	Vince & Jenny Gill
Little Wonders	Rob Thomas
Love Can Build a Bridge	The Judd's
Over the Rainbow	Eva Cassidy
Peace Be With You	Shaina Noll
Prayer of St Francis	Cecilia
Shores of Avalon	Tina Malia
Somewhere over the Rainbow	Eva Cassidy
Somewhere over the Rainbow	Israel Amakawiwo'ole
The Living Proof	Mary J. Blige
The Prayer	Charlotte Church
The Rose	Bette Midler
There is Only Love	Karen Drucker
There You'll Be	Faith Hill
What a Wonderful World	Eva Cassidy
With my Heart	Sarah Burrill
You Light Up My Life	Bianca Ryan
You raise me up	Josh Groban
You've Got a Friend	Carole King

Spirit-filled

Slow

I Am Connected.

Lisa Bailey Sullivan

ALERT!

- Remember the "Your" in Let Your Yoga Dance. Go at your own speed. If your legs are weak or if you have trouble walking or standing, sit down in a chair. It's not only the dancing that affects your spirit, but it's also the music and how it connects to you that is enlivening and life changing.
- Dance like EVERYONE'S watching. Atta girl!

She finally found her true joy...
it was in the present moment.

(atta girl!)

CHAPTER 26

BEING IN THE MOMENT: MINDFULNESS

"What day is it?" asked Pooh.
"It's today," squeaked Piglet.
"My favourite day," said Pooh.

One of the best tools you can use for slowing down and increasing your happiness is mindfulness: a meditation-based practice in which you focus on the present moment without judgment. With today's fast-past, chaotic lifestyles, many women are constantly multi-tasking and never taking those moments to just let their minds be still.

The many benefits of mindfulness include:

- Grounding
- Relaxing
- Relieves stress
- Decreases anxiety
- Improves mood
- Increases self-esteem
- Helps tap into the inner voice
- Improves teamwork
- Increases creativity/productivity
- Increases receptivity to new ideas

Jon Kabat-Zinn is probably the most well-known researcher and leader in teaching mindfulness techniques and benefits. It's increasingly being used in companies, schools,

Here are three different types of mindfulness you can try.

Mindfulness Meditation

Here's basic mindfulness meditation. It's what we talked about during the first chapter:

- Sit in a straight-backed chair or comfortably on the floor.
- Focus on an aspect of your breathing, such as the sensations of air flowing into your nostrils and out of your mouth or your belly rising and falling.
- Once you've narrowed your concentration, expand your awareness to sounds around you, sensations you're feeling and ideas you're having.
- Embrace each sensation or thought without judgment. If your mind races, return to focusing on your breathing, then expand your awareness again.
- Ideally, practice this meditation for five to ten minutes or longer daily. But any amount will provide benefits. During a stressful time, even one minute of mindfulness will help.

Tips on getting the most out of this practice:

Go with the Flow
Once you establish your concentration, observe the flow of inner thoughts, emotions and bodily sensations without judging them as good or bad.

Pay Attention
Notice without attachment external sensations such as sounds, sights, and touch that make up your moment-to-moment experience. Do not latch onto an idea, emotion, or sensation. Do not get caught up thinking about the past or the future. Instead, watch what comes and goes in your mind. Let it flow. Discover which mental habits produce a feeling of well-being or not.

Stay with It
At times, this process may not seem relaxing at all, but over time it provides a key to greater happiness.

Mindful Listening

This is a way of listening without judgment, criticism or interruption while simultaneously being aware of internal thoughts and reactions that may hinder effective communication.

When you listen mindfully:

- You are fully present
- You can absorb the speaker's entire message
- The speaker feels heard and respected
- You cultivate empathy
- You let go of your reactions and other distractions

How to practice mindful listening:

- Your focus should be on the person you are listening to, without distractions.
- Clear your area. If at home, clear the kitchen table. If at work, mute your phone, computer, printer, and any other electronic device.
- Give yourself time. Take a minute or two to clear your mind before you meet with someone. Practice a few relaxation techniques, such as deep breathing, before the conversation.
- Empty your mind of clutter, so you can make room for others' points of view.

Mindful Eating

You can use mindfulness at the table, too. Mindful eating is paying attention to what you're eating, noticing your thoughts, feelings, and sensations, with no judgment.

How to practice mindful eating:

- Eat more slowly and don't rush
- Chew thoroughly
- Feel the texture, taste of each bite
- Eat in silence
- Focus on how the food makes you feel
- Stop eating when you're full

Whatever mindfulness practice you choose, remember it's simply focusing on being in the present without judgment.

Happy Act
Practice Mindfulness

Make a plan to incorporate mindfulness into your life for a week to start.

- Wake up early enough each morning so that you can spend ten minutes breathing in quiet.
- Download a mindfulness app. (I use the Calm app. It's wonderful at helping you establish a practice of mindfulness. It also includes ways to sleep better, master classes on happiness and more.)

When you're practicing being more present, don't forget to be kind to yourself.
Atta girl!

 **ALERT!**

- If you cannot practice mindfulness every day, see how you can incorporate it into your life even just once a week. Remember, get rid of the all-or-nothing mentality. No judgment!

She realized she had enough.

(atta girl!)

CHAPTER 27

GIVING THANKS: GRATITUDE

> "Gratitude makes sense of our past, brings peace
> for today, and creates a vision for tomorrow."
> —Melody Beattie

Gratitude is the quality of being thankful for something or someone. It's appreciation for the good in your life. Robert Emmons, the world's leading scientific expert on gratitude, says gratitude has two key components:

- It's an affirmation of goodness. We affirm that there are good things in the world, gifts, and the benefits that we've received.
- We recognize that the sources of this goodness are outside of ourselves. We acknowledge that other people gave us many gifts, big and small, to help us achieve the goodness in our lives.

Gratitude is a wonderful way to focus on all the positive things and people in your life. In a world where so many around you choose to find fault in everything, it's also one of the most important things you can do for your spirit.

- Gratitude is cost-effective It's free, quick and available to everyone.
- Gratitude increases self-esteem, enhances willpower, strengthens relationships, deepens spirituality, boosts creativity, and improves athletic and academic performance.

- You do not necessarily need to practice gratitude daily. Studies have shown that those who wrote down what they were grateful for just once a week enjoyed the benefit of being happier.

There are many ways to practice gratitude:

- Buy a gratitude journal. Each night write down three to five things that happened that day that you're grateful for.
- Buy a glass bowl or jar. Each night write down one good thing that happened that day that made you smile or that you appreciated. Put it in the bowl. At the end of the year, you'll have 365 records of actual happiness in your life.
- Put a 2-by-3 poster board on your wall. Each time something happens that you're grateful for, write it down in colorful markers. At the end of a few months or a year, you'll have a vivid poster of your gratitude-filled life.
- Go on a gratitude walk. Notice what's around you, like the blue sky above or the kids playing on the street.
- Write a letter of gratitude to someone.
- Send a positive e-mail or text praising or thanking one person you know.
- Do a random act of kindness for a stranger. Giving is the best way to receive.
- Post notes and quotes around your home that remind you to focus on the positive.

How to get the most out of practicing gratitude:

- Do it daily, weekly, or when it feels right
- Introduce variety. For example, if you're grateful for your baby, focus on your baby's smile, then the way he walks. Write something different each time.
- Make it heartfelt. Don't just go through the motions; feel it.
- Visualize it when you write it

Tips on practicing gratitude:

- Buy a gratitude journal
- Whether you like writing what you're grateful for in the morning or at night, it's your choice. There's no right or wrong time.
- Carry a small notebook or use your smartphone. When something happens that you are grateful for, write it down immediately.

Happy Act
Practice Gratitude

Spend two minutes a day scanning your life for three new things you're grateful for. When you do this, you're training your brain to work in a new pattern. Try it now:

1) _____

2) _____

3) _____

Doing this is the fastest way of "teaching" optimism. It will only work if you're scanning for new things and you're very specific. If you say, "I'm grateful for my son," it doesn't work. But if you say, "I'm grateful for my son because he hugged me today, which means I'm loved regardless," then that specificity gets the brain operating in a new pattern of optimism.

Just remember to really *feel* the gratitude.

Atta girl!

**ALERT!**

- If you've heard that you must write down your gratitudes each day, a reprieve is on your way. Research has shown that writing occasional gratitudes (1-3 times per week) is as or more beneficial than daily journaling. The reason is that "having" to write them down each night can feel like a chore and takes away the result. The key is "feeling" the gratitude. Don't force it.
- If writing down what you're grateful feels like a chore, stop! Find other ways to tap into gratitude, such as just noticing and appreciating when something good happens or telling someone what you appreciate about them.
- Become a benefit finder. Reread Chapter 16.

She looked inside and found her superpower.

(atta girl!)

CHAPTER 28

FINDING YOUR SUPERPOWERS: CHARACTER STRENGTHS

"She remembered who she was and the game changed."
—Lalah Deliah

One of my all-time favorite tools in positive psychology is working with your character strengths.

Character strengths are the positive qualities that come naturally to you, such as love, hope, creativity, and fairness. They impact the way you think, feel and behave in all aspects of your life.

Character strengths are part of your core identity and who you are. Research has shown that when you focus on what works — your strengths — you become happier, more engaged and energized. You have a sense of purpose.

Most important, by focusing on your strengths, you view yourself for who you are and not what others want you to be. You focus on what is good and strong about yourself, rather than any problems or weaknesses. It helps you feel empowered and encouraged.

There are 24 character strengths, which are listed at the end of this chapter. Each strength falls under six broad virtues: wisdom, courage, humanity, justice, temperance, and transcendence. Each of us has the 24 strengths, but in varying degrees, forming our unique character profile.

Finding Your Strengths

How do you know what your strengths are? Take the VIA Character Strengths Survey created by the VIA Institute on Character, a nonprofit organization dedicated to bringing the science of character strengths to the world.

The survey is a simple self-assessment that provides a wealth of information to help you understand your core characteristics. Most personality tests focus on negative and neutral traits, but the VIA Survey focuses on your best qualities.

The test is available at viacharacter.org and consists of 240 questions. It will take around 20 minutes to complete. There are no right or wrong answers. You can take the survey at viacharacter.org.

Using Your Strengths

Once you know your strengths, look at your top five strengths. These are your signature strengths. Focusing on your strengths helps you become happier and more successful.

Signature Strengths: Top 5

Your signature strengths are the five strengths that best describe your most positive aspects. Your family and friends would probably agree that these are your top strengths, too. Finding ways to use and express these strengths is likely to bring you many benefits and can help you create your best life.

Middle Strengths: 6-19

Your middle strengths are also an important part of who you are. While these are not your highest (signature) strengths, they are likely to be ones that you mostly express in one life domain, such as work, instead of across all domains. They could also be situational strengths, in that you express them when the circumstance calls for it. These strengths are likely not as automatic as your signature strengths, but they are at your disposal. Focusing on these strengths and building on them can help you in situational aspects of life.

Lesser Strengths: Lower 5
These are character strengths that do not occur as naturally as your other strengths. It probably requires a fair amount of effort and energy for you to use these strengths well. At times, this may even drain you. It's natural to have an interest in giving these lesser strengths a boost. This can be achieved through deliberate practice and by using your signature strengths to support this development.

Happy Act
Use Your Strengths

One way to increase your happiness is to focus on a signature strength and use it.

Answer the following questions.

One of my top strengths is: _____

One thing I will do this week to focus on that strength is:

_____

_____

_____

_____

When you focus on what you love about yourself, you can lead a more fulfilled, happier life.
Atta girl!

 **ALERT!**

- There are <u>no</u> bad strengths. Some women look at their top strengths and think they aren't "fun." Focus on the ones that bring you joy and that you love.
- For ways you can focus on a strength, download a list at lisabaileysullivan.com/happyacts.

Here's a chart of the 24 character strengths as a reference. Why dogs? This is from a happiness tool I created called The Dogma Deck®. The Dogma Deck is modeled after my final project in positive psychology when I was becoming certified. Positive psychology is about focusing on happiness, well-being, and positivity. It's about focusing on what is working in your life, not what isn't working. When you focus on the positive, you become happier. No other living creature on earth is happier than a dog.

Character Strengths
6 Virtues — 24 Character Strengths

Virtue of **Courage** *(strength of heart)*	Bravery	Honesty	Perseverance	Zest

| Virtue of **Humanity** *(strength of others)* | Kindness | Love | Social Intelligence |

| Virtue of **Justice** *(strength of community)* | Fairness  | Leadership | Teamwork |

| Virtue of **Temperance** *(strength of self)* | Forgiveness | Humility | Prudence | Self-Regulation |

| Virtue of **Transcendence** *(strength of spirit)* | Appreciation of Beauty & Excellence | Gratitude | Hope | Humor | Spirituality |

| Virtue of **Wisdom** *(strength of head)* | Creativity | Curiosity | Judgment | Love of Learning | Perspective |

She realized the smallest things
took up the most room in her heart.

(atta girl!)

CHAPTER 29

LOVING-KINDNESS MEDITATION

"If we learn to open our hearts, anyone, including the
people who drive us crazy, can be our teacher."
—Pema Chödrön

Loving-kindness meditation, also called metta meditation, is the simple practice of directing well-wishes and goodwill towards yourself and others through silent mantras.

In a landmark study, Barbara Frederickson, a psychology professor at the University of North Carolina, and her colleagues found that practicing seven weeks of the loving-kindness meditation increased love, joy, contentment, gratitude, pride, hope, interest, amusement, and awe.

WOW! Who wouldn't want all of that?!

It's also a particularly effective practice if you are holding a grudge against someone or feel like someone has wronged you and you don't quite know how to tap into forgiveness.

Another research study showed that a single seven-minute loving-kindness meditation made people feel more loving and accepting of themselves and more connected to and positive about loved ones and total strangers.

To begin this practice, find a quiet place where you can focus on your thoughts for five to ten minutes.

1. Start by directing these phrases towards yourself.

   - May I be happy.
   - May I be well.
   - May I be safe.
   - May I be at peace and live in ease.

2. Next, direct the same sentiments towards someone you feel thankful for or love.

   - May _____be happy.
   - May _____be well.
   - May _____be safe.
   - May _____be at peace and live in ease.

3. Now, visualize someone you feel neutral about — a person you neither like nor dislike. This one can be difficult, as it shows how quickly we judge people as either positive or negative in our lives.

   - May _____be happy.
   - May _____be well.
   - May _____be safe.
   - May _____be at peace and live in ease.

4. The next one may be easier: visualizing someone you're having a difficult time with or don't like. Maybe it's someone you wish you could forgive but just can't.

   - May _____be happy.
   - May _____be well.
   - May _____be safe.
   - May _____be at peace and live in ease.

5.   Finally, direct the metta towards everyone universally:

- May all beings be happy.
- May all beings be well.
- May all beings be safe.
- May all beings be at peace and live in ease.

Doing this simple yet powerful loving-kindness meditation can make you feel less isolated and more connected to those around you.

Happy Act
Practice Metta

For one week, practice the loving-kindness meditation. At the end of the period, see how you feel about yourself and a person you are struggling with. You're on your way to making metta a part of your life.

Atta girl!

 **ALERT!**

- When it comes to loving-kindness, there's not a single item to alert you to!

She bloomed wherever she was planted.

(atta girl!)

CHAPTER 30

THE 30-DAY PRACTICE

'The question isn't who's going to let me; it's who is going to stop me."
—Ayn Rand

Throughout this book, I've shared what I hope are many useful tools. They are intended to help you become that woman you were born to be. But sometimes, it takes a nudge to get started. This is where a 30-day practice comes in.

This is about trying something new, different, fun, or even crazy every day for 30 days. Large or small, what matters is that consistent action is taken. Small daily actions build behaviors and habits that stick.

Why 30 days? To change anything, you have to change your behavior. Practicing for 30 days helps you to develop new habits. You learn you can change your life by changing your days.

Why not kick things off next month? Start small, like taking a walk, taking a nature picture, reading a poem every day, or visualizing who you want to be for five minutes every day. Just do one thing. The key is not to overwhelm yourself. Remember baby steps.

Then, after the first 30 days, start another 30-day practice. Keep going!

Atta girl!

Happy Act
Your 30-Day Practice

Complete the following:

For the next 30 days, I will do this: _____

_____

_____

**ALERT!**

- If, for some reason you're not able to do this for 30 consecutive days, you must give yourself <u>permission to be human. And try again.</u> Atta girl!

FINAL ART

WHAT REALLY MATTERS

Sh*tshow

noun. (U.S. slang) offensive, very informal

1: A PERFECT STORM OF EVERYTHING GOING WRONG
— One unexpected, life-changing sh*tshow of an incident caused her to focus on fear and worry.

What Really Matters

expression. truth.

1. SH*TSHOWS HAPPEN, YOU'LL GET THROUGH THEM — She took a deep breath, did a little dancing, persevered, embraced her power, used her outside voice, stopped caring what others think, rediscovered her true-self, and shined on.

(atta girl!)

Final Art: What Really Matters

If All Else Fails

If you're knee-deep in the middle of a sh*tshow, you probably don't have time to read. So, if that's you (and I've been there with you!), just read the final two chapters.

Atta girl!

She lived her life with a cherry on top.

(atta girl!)

CHAPTER 31

HOLY CRAP! FINAL ALERTS!

I hope you've enjoyed the Turd Alerts! throughout this book, highlighting what you need to know at the end of each chapter. They've been among my favorite parts to write. Here are the final alerts, covering some of my favorites with a few, er, little nuggets of additional wisdom.

ALERT!

- Breathe.
- If someone asks you if you are happy, run away. No one is happy all the time.
- No one lives fearlessly all the time. No one. And that's okay.
- Give yourself permission to be human. Feel free to experience all emotions. If you ignore or suppress anger, sadness, jealousy, fear, or frustration, these emotions will only intensify.
- Give back. Find your purpose. It will help you become happier and more fulfilled.
- Wake up early. Listen to that morning breeze. Know you are not going at this alone.
- Make fear your friend, don't run from it. Name it. Embrace it. Friend it. Then kick its a** to the curb.

- Find your voice and use it. Make your ask be louder than your fear.
- USE YOUR OUTSIDE VOICE.
- Let go of things that don't serve you. Let that sh*t go. The Universe won't give you something new until you get rid of the stuff that no longer serves you.
- Don't get caught in the middle of someone's sh*t. Let that sh*t go, too. Let that sh*t(show) go.
- As one of my best friends advised: Disregard random negatives. Don't be dragged into a sh*tshow because of some random comment by someone who is just unhappy and wants to drag others with her.
- Know it's OK to change directions. You can always begin again. Always.
- It's okay to tell someone NO, even yourself.
- Think deeply about what your priorities are in life. Say yes to what connects to your priorities and say no to everything else.
- Look for the benefits. We all have peaks and valleys. Even the valleys have important lessons.
- Forgiveness doesn't mean forgetting. And forgiveness is on your timetable, not someone else's.
- Forgiving yourself is the most important forgiveness of all. Like everyone else, you're just trying to find your way in your sometimes-crazy life.
- There are no failures. You're just discovering new ways to do what you want to do.
- When your head hits the bed each night, think only of positive thoughts. Before you put your feet on the ground in the morning, think only of positive thoughts.
- Ask yourself each morning, "What can I do to love myself a little more today?" Then, do it.
- Be kind. Be kind to yourself and others. If you have the choice to be right or be kind, choose kind. Life isn't a battle to be won and love is more than just a word.
- Focus on your "get to do's" as much as your "have to do's." And realize you can turn some of your "have to do's" into "get to do's."

- Talk to yourself like you would talk to your best friend or child. Practice positive I AMs.
- Rip off those negative labels.
- Find your tribe, women who lift you up. And if you can't find your tribe yet, be your own best friend. Your tribe will appear when it's supposed to.
- Don't look back, you're not going that way.
- Discover and live your adventure, not someone else's.
- Step out of your comfort zone. You'll only regret the chances you didn't take, not the ones you did.
- Always remember: You. Are. NOT. Too. Old. It's never too late to be who you want to be or do what you want to do.
- Keep it real. You do you. As long as you do you, the world is yours.
- Be open to everything and attached to nothing.
- Remember the law of attraction: what you put out is what you attract.
- Play! Don't take life or your desires so seriously. The more you play and detach, the more the Universe brings you.
- LAUGH. LAUGH. LAUGH!
- DANCE! DANCE! DANCE! (Like everyone's watching.)
- Go outside as much as you can. Walk among the trees.
- Greatness is not about being better than anyone else. It's about being better than you used to be.
- Stop living your life based on the opinions of others. STOP. CARING. WHAT. OTHERS. THINK. OF. YOU.
- Believe in something greater than yourself. Call it God, Spirit, Universe, Source or even Pikachu, it doesn't matter. Just know there is a loving, protective force with you always.
- When all else fails, buy yourself a boat horn, stand in the middle of the sh*tshow, blast the horn, say "F" it and walk away.
- Breathe.

Atta girl.

She realized she was all she needed.

(atta girl!)

CHAPTER 32

AFTERWORD
Fuggedaboudit: The Most Important Chapter of Them All

If you are a woman (and again, if you're reading this, I'm thinking you're a woman), you probably took a dance lesson or two when you were little.

I jumped into the dancing lesson "rite of passage" and took my first dance lessons when I was four years old.

While I have fond memories of learning how to dance, two things stand out to me from that experience. First, at the beginning of each class, we'd sit in a circle with a pair of castanets and sing, "Happy Talk." Second, my first recital consisted of tap dancing to "Put on a Happy Face."

One of my favorite childhood pictures is of me from before that very recital. I'm holding a hat with a creepy happy face, which I would reveal to the audience when I bowed during the chorus.

I don't look happy in that picture and the irony makes me smile. Back then, no one was going to tell me to be happy if I didn't want to be. I'm still that way today.

Like me, no one can tell you to be happy and no one can make you happy. Singing a song about being happy is not going to do it. Taking a course on positive psychology is not going to do it. Reading a book on how to live fearlessly happy through all your sh*tshows is not going to do it.

Learning to live fearlessly happy is a personal journey for everyone. Your happiness comes from your own little "carefully curated ensemble of the science and the woo-woo" you've gathered throughout your life. It comes from all the lessons you've learned from all the sh*tshows you've sat through.

Here's why I have written this book:

- I want you to live your best life.
- I want you to be who you were born to be.
- I want you to stop caring about what others think and start caring about what you think.
- I want you to love yourself so deeply that barbs and arrows thrown from others bounce off and fall silently to the ground.
- I want you to find and use your voice.
- I want you to realize the power you have to be whatever it is you want to be.
- I want to help you realize that it's never too late to:
    o Rediscover that playful, happy girl inside
    o Be the person you are meant to be
    o Do what you feel called to do
    o Shine your light and turn the world on with your smile. (I say this with my deep appreciation for the opening song of the Mary Tyler Moore Show.)
- I want you to live a life that's filled with fun and joy every day!
- I want you to do you.
- I want you to play BIG.

I hope that by sharing all that I've learned on my journey to living fearlessly happy, it can help you live fearlessly happy, too — no matter the sh*tshow.

If something in this book resonates with you and does help you, that's wonderful! I've accomplished my goal.

But if nothing does, that's okay, too. In fact, fuggedaboudit. All of it. Just ignore what I've written.

Instead, turn to you. What's in your heart? What's your inner voice telling you?

Whatever *that* is, that's what's going to get you through any sh*tshow.

Your inner voice is that little girl telling you to take a deep breath and just be you.

Because when you finally start being who God, Spirit, your higher power or you intended you to be, when you finally start being truly yourself, that's when you'll tap into your power and moxie and start on the path to living fearlessly happy.

You do you.

Atta girl.

Grateful for….

ACKNOWLEDGMENTS AND RESOURCES

So many people and organizations have had an incredible impact on me and guided me on my personal journey to living fearlessly happy. I am grateful for their teachings, mentorship, and friendship, which have contributed so much to this book.

Megha Nancy Buttenheim and Let Your Yoga Dance®

Total gratitude to my favorite mentor, Megha Nancy Buttenheim, M.A., E-RYT 1000 and CJO (Chief JOY Officer) of Let Your Yoga Dance.

Megha is the Founding Director of Let Your Yoga Dance and author of "Expanding Joy: Let Your Yoga Dance, Embodying Positive Psychology." She is also an international presenter, who's led teacher trainings, retreats and classes since 1985. She brings her passion and expertise as a lifelong dancer, actress, singer, yogi and educator in experiential learning to all her workshops and trainings. To see all that she offers, visit letyouryogadanc.com and meghanancybuttenheim.com.

Thank you to Irena Blethen, who oversees the Let Your Yoga Dance Teachers Association. She put together a wonderful list of songs to help with this practice, many of which are included in the song lists in the Happy Beginnings section.

Wholebeing Institute

Special thanks to the Wholebeing Institute, where I was certified in positive psychology. I've learned many valuable tools from them, including their SPIRE Model for Wellbeing and Happiness. For more information, visit wholebeinginstitute.com.

Tal Ben-Shahar

Special thanks to Tal Ben-Shahar — a teacher and writer in the areas of positive psychology and leadership. As a Harvard University lecturer, Ben-Shahar created the most popular course in school's history, Positive Psychology and The Psychology of Leadership. He is the co-creator of SPIRE and creator of the Happiness Studies Academy. For more information, visit happinessstudies.academy.

Other Teachers and Mentors

This carefully curated ensemble of the science and the woo-woo includes so much of what I've read and learned from others. If I've quoted someone incorrectly or neglected to quote you, this is unintentional. Please contact me so I may correct this in future editions.

My Former Employers

This book wouldn't have been possible without you and our shared experiences and valuable lessons. I am so grateful for each of those experiences and lessons, more than you know. Thank you.

Earth, Wind, and Fire

A special thank you to all the powerful and amazing women who have touched my heart throughout my life. There are so many people who have had my back, who have been there for me, and who have made me laugh and smile just by being the beautiful souls they are. I especially want to thank Earth, Wind and Fire. No, not the group (although their songs are some of my favorites to dance to!). EW&F are my pen names for three women who have gotten me through more sh*tshows than I can count.

Kathy Walsh

My extreme gratitude for my editor, Kathy Walsh, who not only edited this carefully curated ensemble of the science and the woo-woo, but also supported me through the entire process of writing it.

My Sisters

We don't have the typical relationship that most sisters have. It's not easy being the youngest of 3 girls, but I also know it's not easy being the oldest or the middle. We each have our own experiences, stories, and truths. But I see wisdom, kindness, power, moxie and beauty in each of them.

My Mom

She passed ten years ago. I never truly appreciated her strength and moxie when she was living. It took going through my own challenges over the past few years to fully realize just how strong and amazing she was. Thank you, Mom. You taught me well. Atta girl, Barb! Atta girl!

Helpful Books and Websites:

- "Change Your Thoughts, Change Your Life" — Wayne Dyer
- "The Power of Intention" — Wayne Dyer
- "Happier" — Tal Ben-Shahar
- "Full Catastrophe Living" — Jon Kabat-Zinn
- "Thanks! How the New Science of Gratitude Can Make You Happier" — Robert A. Emmons
- "The Little Book of Gratitude" — Robert A. Emmons
- "Character Strengths Interventions: A Field Guide for Practitioners" — Ryan Niemiec
- The Calm App
- letyouryogadance.com
- meghanancybuttenheim.com
- tut.com
- nexttribe.com
- growingbolder.com
- thetappingsolution.com
- viacharacter.org

More Websites

I have my own websites and more helpful tools that I'd love to share with you.

- campattagirl.com — retreats for women who want to play BIG!
- lisabaileysullivan.com & happinesselement.com — bringing the science of happiness to companies and organizations
- bartandlisa.com — a site my husband and I created to share humor and wisdom

ABOUT THE AUTHOR

Lisa Bailey Sullivan

Lisa is a wife, mom, experienced corporate marketing exec, happiness activist and the CHO (chief happiness officer) of her crazy-happy life. Most of all, she's someone who wants to lighten up the world and help others become more positive and optimistic and realize their full potential.

Drawing from the latest science from positive psychology and with more than two decades of corporate marketing leadership experience, Lisa offers simple, tested actions that can help reduce stress and anxiety and cultivate a lasting sense of wellbeing and happiness at work and in life.

She is certified in positive psychology through The Wholebeing Institute and a graduate of the Happiness Studies Academy, studying under Tal Ben-Shahar, an educator and leader in positive psychology. She has attended Google's Search Inside Yourself training. Lisa is also a certified trainer of Mike Dooley's Infinite Possibilities: The Art of Living Your Dreams and a certified teacher in Let Your Yoga Dance, an amazing, joy-filled power dance combining yoga, breath and user-friendly dance with fabulous music from across the world.

She created Camp Atta Girl!™ — day and overnight retreats that help women realize it's never too late to rediscover that playful, happy girl inside and be that person she is meant to be. Her intention is to help every woman find her joy, voice, power, and self-love, so that she has the courage to do what she feels called to do.

Along with producing Camp Atta Girl! and other ways to help women play big, she brings the tools of positive psychology to companies and organizations to help employees experience greater happiness at work.

You can learn more about her and her work here:

- campattagirl.com — retreats for women who want to embrace their power, voice, and joy and play BIG in life!
- lisabaileysullivan.com
- happinesselement.com — bringing the science of happiness to companies and organizations
- bartandlisa.com — featuring a couple's humor and wisdom

ENDNOTES

1 Special thanks to Lois Kelly, who in her infinite wisdom wrote three simple words in one of her blogs: slam it down. Lois is an author, facilitator, communications strategist and a rebel. You can learn more about her great work and wild spirit at foghound.com

2 Tal Ben-Shahar is an author and lecturer. He taught two of the largest classes in Harvard University's history, Positive Psychology and The Psychology of Leadership. Today, Tal consults and lectures around the world to executives in multi-national corporations, the general public, and at-risk populations. The topics he lectures on include leadership, happiness, education, innovation, ethics, self-esteem, resilience, goal setting, and mindfulness. He is the co-creator of SPIRE and creator of the Happiness Studies Academy. For more information, visit happinessstudies.academy and talbenshahar.com.

3 Megha Nancy Buttenheim, M.A., is the founder and CJO (Chief Joy Officer) of Let Your Yoga Dance®. An international presenter, Megha has been leading teacher-trainings, retreats, and classes at Kripalu Center in Stockbridge, Massachusetts since 1985. She brings her passion and expertise as a lifelong dancer, actress, singer, yogi, and educator in experiential learning to all her workshops and trainings. Her mission, for over 30 years, has been to bring "Healing through Joy" to the world while demonstrating that "Everyone is a Dancer." For more information, visit meghanancybuttenheim.com

4 Stacy Davenport is an experienced, dynamic and insightful certified Feng Shui expert, development Coach, educator and author. She has spent more than two decades coaching individuals and business leaders on how to create positive change within their lives and their businesses. For more information, visit stacydavenport.com.

5 The Wholebeing Institute was founded by Megan McDonough & Tal Ben-Shahar (mentioned previously). Megan is an award-winning author of Infinity in a Box and A Minute for Me. With a degree in nuclear medicine, senior leadership experience in health care, two decades as a yoga practitioner and teacher, and experience directing numerous online-learning start-ups, Megan focuses on how to get from point A to point B through whole-person

engagement. She is also the General Manager of Kripalu's RISE program. For more information, visit wholebeinginstitute.com.

6   Jean Jyotika Skeels is a writer, poet, dancer, photographer, wife, mother and nurturer to those journeying through the fertile void. She has a voice that speaks to the soul and a spirit that helps those around her feel a sense of friendship, community, beauty and sacredness. She specializes in life companioning, helping those who are seeking a companion to push through life's challenges. You can reach her at jeanskeels.com.

She doesn't care what people think of her
because she's too busy.

She's got magical sh*t to do.

(atta girl!)

Printed in the United States
By Bookmasters